Anne E. Garnier

Gossip from a muniment room:

Being passages in the lives of Anne and Mary Fytton, 1574-1618

Anne E. Garnier

Gossip from a muniment room:
Being passages in the lives of Anne and Mary Fytton, 1574-1618

ISBN/EAN: 9783337810757

Printed in Europe, USA, Canada, Australia, Japan

Cover: Foto ©ninafisch / pixelio.de

More available books at **www.hansebooks.com**

GOSSIP FROM A
MUNIMENT ROOM

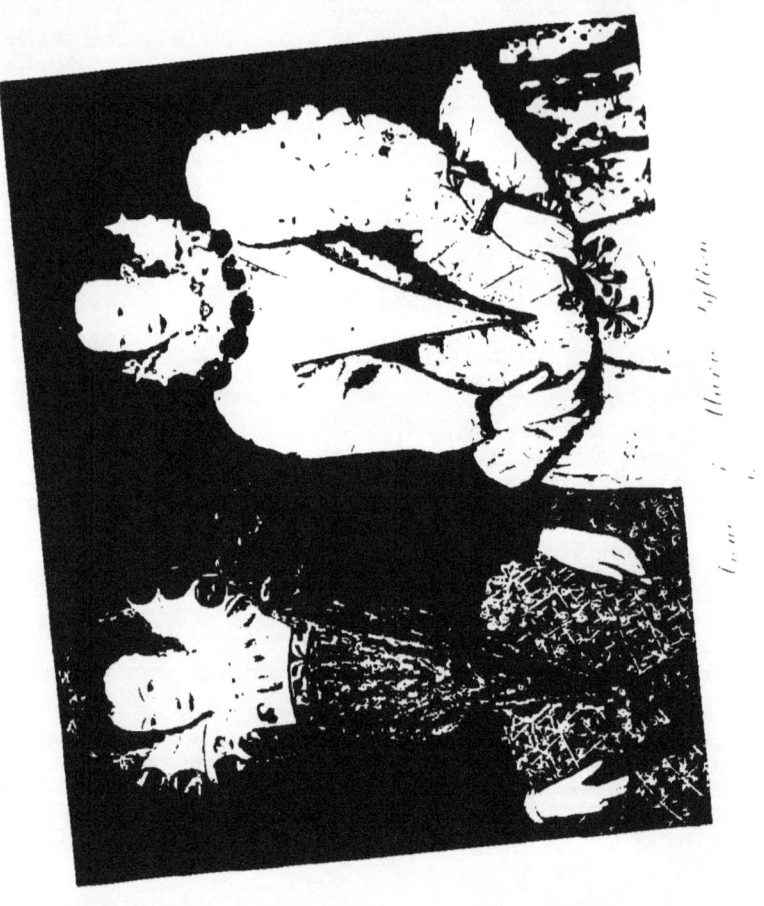

GOSSIP FROM A MUNIMENT ROOM

BEING PASSAGES IN THE LIVES
OF ANNE AND MARY FYTTON
1574 TO 1618

TRANSCRIBED AND EDITED BY
LADY NEWDIGATE-NEWDEGATE

LONDON: DAVID NUTT IN THE
STRAND   MDCCCXCVII

TO MY HUSBAND

LT.-GENERAL

Sir EDWARD NEWDIGATE-NEWDEGATE, K.C.B.

OF ARBURY

AND

GREAT-GREAT-GREAT-GREAT-GREAT-GRANDSON

OF ANNE FYTTON

LADY NEWDIGATE

INTRODUCTION

THE following passages in the lives of Anne and Mary Fytton have been chiefly gleaned from old letters and papers in the Muniment Room at Arbury. The task of putting them together in the form of a narrative was undertaken in the first instance for the benefit of the descendants of the elder sister, who have hitherto known little about her. It has since been suggested that so genuine and authentic a record of that distant period may have a wider interest than for family only.

The history of Anne is of necessity a one-sided tale, being

Introduction

being drawn from the large correspondence she kept up with both men and women friends after her marriage, and though she carefully preserved their letters, her own, with one or two exceptions, are not at hand to make the narrative as complete as could be desired.

Mary Fytton, on the other hand, is not unknown to history, and some interest has been aroused in her of late years by Mr. Tyler's clever attempt to identify her with the Dark Ladye of "Shakspeare's Sonnets."*

On one point there is ample evidence. Both sisters seem to have been unusually gifted with physical and mental charms, and to have been admired and loved by persons of note in the era in which they lived.

In order to make this account more complete and interesting, the letters will not be given in their bald simplicity, but with explanatory connecting links and with short biographical and historical facts concerning the writers.

The letters will follow each other as far as possible in their proper sequence, but where there are no dates it is only from internal evidence that they can be placed in their supposed order.

The

* See Tyler's "Shakspeare's Sonnets." David Nutt, Strand.

Introduction

The spelling is preserved as written, though of the most varied character, even the proper names in signatures and addresses differing as the writer's phonetic sense dictates.

It is unavoidable that occasional references and observations in these letters remain unexplained. As mentioned above, the clue which might be given by the other side of the correspondence is absent. In spite of this drawback, we shall hope to give a fairly consecutive history of some twenty-two years in the lives of our heroines, inventing nothing and withholding neither good nor evil, though the frankness of one or two of the writers is somewhat startling to modern ideas.

CONTENTS

Chapter I

Court & Country Life . . . . Page 1

Anne's Marriage—Letter of Arabella Stewart—Mary becomes Maid of Honour—Sir William Knollys' Letters—Anne's Daughter Born—Sir Fulke Greville's Letters.

Chapter II

Mary's Downfall & Disgrace . . . 26

Sir W. Knollys' Letters—Troubles at Court—Mary in Disgrace—Dismissal from her Post—Sir W. Knollys' Letters.

Chapter III

The Leveson Letters 48

Sir Richard Leveson's Letters—Sir Fulke Greville's Letters—Death of Queen Elizabeth—Sir John Newdigate Knighted—Sir R. Leveson's Letters—His Death and Will.

Contents

Chapter IV

Widowhood 71

    Mary's Manner of Life—Her Marriage—Sir Fulke Greville's Letters—His Death—Mary's Widowhood—Death of Sir John Newdigate—Anne's Petitions for the Wardship of her Son.

Chapter V

Friendship 92

    Letters from Francis Beaumont to Anne Newdigate.

Chapter VI

Courtship 112

    Cosyn Saunders and his Suit—Francis Beaumont's Letters—Final Dismissal of Cosyn Saunders—Mary's Second Marriage.

Chapter VII

The Valley of Death 135

    Letters from Lady Grey—Anne's Cares for her Children—Her Declining Health—Her Death and her Will.

SKETCH PEDIGREE OF NEWDIGATES AND FYTTONS.

John Newdegate, of Harefield, co. Middlesex, Esq., King's Serjeant 12 Hen. VIII., *d.* 16 August 1528, bur. at Harefield. = Amphilis, dau. and heir of John Nevill, Esq., of Mabelthorpe (and son of Sir Thomas Nevill, of Holt, co. Leicester, and Rolleston, co. Notts, Kt.), *d.* 15 July 1544, bur. at Harefield.

John Newdegate, of Harefield, Esq., *d.* 19 June 1545, bur. at Harefield. = Ann, dau. and heir of Nicholas Hilton, of co. York, bur. at Harefield, 9 March 1546–7.

John Newdegate, of Harefield, Esq., *b.* 9 Oct. 1513, M.P. for Middlesex, 1553, 1554, and 1558; *m.* (2) Elizabeth, dau. of Thomas Lovett of Astwell, co. Northants, and widow of Anthony Cave, of Chicheley, Esq., bur. at Harefield, 20 Aug. 1565. = Mary, dau. of Sir Robert Cheney, of Chesham Boys, co. Bucks, Kt. (1st wife).

John Newdegate, of Harefield, Esq., *b.* 5 Feb. 1541 2, exchanged Harefield for Arbury, co. Warwick, 20 Nov. 1585; *m.* (2) *circ.* 1575-6, Mary Smith, and (3) *circ.* 1577, Winifred Wells, bur. 26 Feb. 1591-2. = Martha, dau. and coheiress of Anthony Cave, Esq., of Chicheley, co. Bucks, *b.* 24 Feb. 1545–6, bur. at Harefield, 22 Nov. 1575 (1st wife).

Sir Edward Fytton, of Gawsworth, co. Chester, Kt., *b. circ.* 1500, Sheriff of Cheshire, 1532 and 1534, *d.* 17 Feb. 1547 8. = Mary, dau. and co-heiress of Sir Guiscard Harbottle, Kt., of co. Northumberland, *d.* 12 Dec. 1556.

Sir Edward Fytton, Kt., *b.* 31 March 1527, Lord President of Connaught and Thomond, Treasurer of Ireland, *d.* 3 July 1579, bur. Dublin Cathedral. = Anne, dau. of Sir Peter Warburton, Kt., of Arley, co. Chester, *b.* 1 May 1527, *m.* 19 Jan. 1539-40, *d.* 9 Jan. 1573 4, bur. Dublin Cathedral.

Francis Fytton, Esq., of Wadhorough, co. Worcester, *m.* 1588, Katherine, dau. and co-heiress of John Nevill, Lord Latimer, and widow of Henry, 8th Earl of Northumberland, *d.s.p.* 17 June 1608.

Mary, *b.* 1529, *d.* 27 July 1591. = Sir Richard Leveson, Kt., of Trentham, co. Staffs, and Lilleshall, co. Salop, *d.* 1559.

Sir Walter Leveson, Kt., *d.* 1602. = Anne, dau. of Sir Andrew Corbet, Kt., of Moreton Corbet, co. Salop.

Sir Richard Leveson, Kt., Vice-Admiral, *b. circ.* 1569, *m.* 1587, Lady Margaret Howard, dau. of Earl of Nottingham, *d.s.p.* 2 Aug. 1605.

Sir Edward Fytton, Kt., *b. circ.* 1550, Lord President of Munster, M.P. for Boroughbridge, 1588–9, *d.* 4 March 1605–6, bur. at Gawsworth. = Alice, dau. and coheiress of Sir John Holcroft, of Holcroft, co. Lancaster, Kt., bur. at Gawsworth, 4 Jan. 1616 7.

Alexander Fytton, Captain in the army, of Awrice, co. Limerick, in 1634, *m.* Jane, dau. of MacBryan O'Connagh. His son, William, and grandson, Sir Alexander, L.C. of Ireland, as heir male of the Fyttons, had lawsuits with Lord Gerard of Brandon, about Gawsworth estate.

Sir John Newdigate, Kt., *b.* 5 March 1570–1, knighted 23 July 1603, *d.* 28 March, and bur. at Harefield, 12 April 1610. = Anne Fytton, bapt. at Gawsworth, 6 October 1574, *m.* at Stepney, 30 April 1587, bur. at Harefield, 22 July 1618.

Sir Edward Fytton, *b.* 29 Nov. 1572, created Baronet 2 Oct. 1617, *d.* 10 May 1619, bur. at Gawsworth. = Anne, dau. and coheiress of James Barrett, of Tenby, co. Pembroke, *b. circ.* 1571, *d.* March 1644.

Richard Fytton, *d.s.p.* in London, bur. at Gawsworth, 5 June 1610.

Mary Fytton, bapt. at Gawsworth, 24 June 1578, Maid of Honour to Queen Elizabeth, 1595, *m.* (1) *circ.* 1607, William Polwheele, Esq., of Perton co. Staffs, who *d.* 1610; *m.* (2) John Lougher, who *d. circ.* 1635. She *d.* 1647, will dated 19 Dec. 1640, proved 1 July 1647. Left issue surviving.

John Newdigate, Esq., *b.* 27 May 1600, Sheriff of Warwickshire, 1626, M.P. for Liverpool, 1628-9, *m.* 1621, Susanna, dau. of Arnold Luls, of London, a Dutch merchant, *d.s.p.* surv., bur. at Harefield, 19 Nov. 1642.

Sir Richard Newdegate, 1st Bart., *b.* 17 Sept. 1602, Serj.-at-law and Judge (of Commonwealth), 1654; C.J. 1660, M.P. for Tamworth, 1660, created Bart. 1677; repurchased Harefield, 1674-75, *d.* 14 Oct. 1678, bur. at Harefield. = Julian, 3rd dau. of Sir Francis Leigh, K.B., of Newnham Regis, co. Warwick, *b. circ.* 1610, *m.* 2 Feb. 1631-32, *d.* 9 Dec. 1685, bur. at Harefield.

Newdigates of Arbury.

Mary, *b.* 7 May 1598, *m.* 2 Feb. 1619–20, Edmund Bolton, Esq. of Granborough, co. Warwick, *d.* 1643.

Lettice, *b.* 3 Nov. 1604, *d.* unmar. bur. at Harefield, 25 March 1625.

Anne, *b.* 16 Oct. 1607, *m.* Sir Rich. Skeffington Kt., *d.* 21 May 1637, bur. at St. Michael's, Coventry.

Sir Edward Fytton, 2nd Bart., bapt. 24 Aug. 1603, Sheriff of Cheshire 1633, *m.* (1), Jane, dau. of Sir John Trevor, Kt., of Plâs Teg, co. Flint, and (2) Felicia, dau. of Ralph Sneyd, Esq., of Keele, co. Staffs, *d.s.p.* surv. Aug. 1643.

Richard, *b.* 1607, *d.* 1608.

Thomas, *b.* 1608, *d.s.p.* 1630.

Penelope (2nd dau.), *b. circ.* 1595, *m.* 12 Jan. 1611 2, Sir Charles Gerard, Kt., of Halsall, co. Lancs. Their son, Charles Gerard, was created Lord Gerard of Brandon and Earl of Macclesfield, and recovered Gawsworth estates after long lawsuit with William Fytton of Awrice, and his son, Sir Alex. Fytton, the heirs male.

CHAPTER I

Court & Country Life

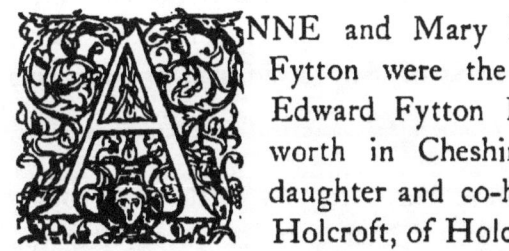NNE and Mary Phyton, Fitton or Fytton were the daughters of Sir Edward Fytton Knight, of Gawsworth in Cheshire, and of Alice, daughter and co-heiress of Sir John Holcroft, of Holcroft in Lancashire. The Fyttons evidently thought much of themselves, and with reason. They were of ancient lineage, had filled posts of honour in the State, and had been knighted for more than one past generation.

Anne, the elder daughter, was born in October 1574, and her only sister Mary some three and a half years later. They had two brothers: the elder, Edward, afterwards a baronet; and the younger, Richard, who died

died unmarried in 1610. Sir Edward, the first baronet, had a daughter, Penelope, who married Sir Charles Gerard. Their son, created Lord Gerard of Brandon, and Earl of Macclesfield, succeeded to the Gawsworth estates on the failure of issue to Penelope Fytton's brother, the second and last baronet.

Anne Fytton, in accordance with the practice of the age, had a husband chosen for her by her parents when she was still a child. At twelve years of age she was married in London to John Newdegate or Newdigate,* aged sixteen, the eldest son of John Newdegate, of Arbury in Warwickshire. The mother of the youthful bridegroom was Martha Cave, daughter and co-heiress of Anthony Cave, of Chichely, Bucks. She died in 1575, a few years after the birth of her son.

Arbury seems to have been securely settled on young John Newdegate. His father married twice after his first wife's death, had several more sons, and accumulated debts to such an extent that he ended his days in the Fleet Prison, dying there at the age of fifty. Nevertheless, he it was who bought Arbury in 1586 from Sir Edmund Anderson, Chief Justice of the Common Pleas in Queen Elizabeth's reign. The present

---

* The name has been spelt in various ways. The present family spell it with an i, excepting the owner of Arbury, who is obliged by will to spell it with an e.

sent house had been built a few years previously by Sir Edmund on the ruins of the old Erdburie Priory. John Newdegate had to give up his old family manor of Harefield, in Middlesex, in part payment for Arbury, retaining only the messuage and farm of Brackenbury, with the chapel of that name forming the south aisle in Harefield Church—the burial-place of his family for many generations. Sir Edmund Anderson soon parted with Harefield to Sir Thomas Egerton (afterwards Baron Ellesmere), Lord Keeper to Queen Elizabeth, who married as his second wife Alice, widow of Ferdinando, Earl of Derby. The manor of Harefield was bought back from the heirs of this Lady Derby by John Newdegate's grandson some ninety years later. Sir Thomas Egerton and his son, Sir John Egerton (afterwards Earl of Bridgewater), married, one the widowed Countess of Derby and the other her second daughter, Lady Frances Stanley, who is mentioned in one of the letters that follow.

After the ceremony of marriage between Anne Fytton and young John Newdigate in 1587, Sir Edward Fytton seems to have undertaken the young couple's expenses. Many years later Anne refers to her father's having kept "her husband, herself, a mayde and two men for nine years after her marriage of freewill and without ever haveing paye allowed."

She appears to have been living at home in her father's house at Gawsworth or in London during this period, whilst

whilst her boy-husband was probably continuing his education elsewhere.

In a letter from John Newdegate (the spendthrift) "to the Right Worshippfull Sir Edward ffytton Knight," dated November 1588, and entirely on money matters, he adds as a postscript, "Good S^r, let me see my daughter, how I longe to see her."

Anne was at this time just fourteen years old.

The earliest portrait of the two sisters at Arbury must have been taken four years later. It is a double one, three-quarter length, and painted on a panel. Their respective ages of eighteen and fifteen are recorded on the picture. Anne, the elder, has dark hair and eyes and arched eyebrows. She has a gentle, serious expression, and is depicted full face, the shape of an oval contour, whilst her features are small and regular. She is dressed in hoop and ruff in accordance with the costume of the period. Mary's girlish figure is less matured, her complexion fairer and her face narrower with a longer nose. Her lively grey eyes have the alert bright look of her age, indicating, perhaps, already the wit and brilliancy which were among her prominent charms.

It must have been whilst Anne was still an inmate of her old home that she became acquainted with the ill-fated Arabella Stuart, or, as she spells her own name, "Arbella Stewart." The two girls were nearly of an age, Anne being one year the older of the two. She has preserved the following letter from her friend, it being

being as remarkable for the extreme beauty of the writing as for its superiority in diction and spelling to others from persons in the same position of life at that period.

It is addressed "To my good frende, Mrs Anne Newdigate."

I thancke you sweet Mrs Newdigate for your fine cuffes and kinde rememberance of me, hopinge this our acquaintance newlye begonne shall continewe, and growe greater hereafter, Of which I shall be uerye gladde; as likewise I shall be to see you somtime here when you best can. Thus with my uery hartye comendations to you and my Lady Fitton, I ende. Chessey this 14 of March.

Your assured frende
ARBELLA STEWART.

It was not until 1595 or 1596 that Anne Newdigate finally left her father's house to begin her married life at Arbury. About the same time Mary Fytton received the appointment of Maid of Honour to Queen Elizabeth. Henceforth Anne's and Mary's paths in life took very different directions, but in joy and sorrow, through good report and evil report, in spite of sin and shame, Anne clung to her sister Mary with faithful affection.

One of the earliest letters preserved by the young wife after she left London is from an old friend who much regrets her departure.

To my honorable fayre M^ris Ann Newdigate theise at Arbery.

Longeinge so much as I doe to heare of yor good agreement wth the Contrye life I have persuaded my Comforteless Eyes to watch tyll my hand might discover my desire to be satisfied therein. Wright wth every occasion soe shall you hence ordinarily receyve salutacons. Noe Newes heare worthy you, all at this end of the towne are become melancholicque for the want of yor presens. I love you and ever will, and soe I betake you to yor rest, beinge about to take my owne.

Strann this present Mundaye, December 1596.

Yo^rs

HEN CARYE.

We cannot make out for certain who the writer of this letter was.* It could not have been Henry Carey, Lord Hunsdon, the first cousin of Queen Elizabeth, for he died in July of that same year; but it was probably some member of this family, as there are letters of the same period from Lord Hunsdon's daughter Margaret, Lady Hoby, with whom Anne Newdigate seems to have been on intimate terms.

We must now leave Anne to accommodate herself to
"the

---

* There was a Sir Henry Cary who was made Master of the Jewels on June 21, 1603, on James I.'s accession.

Court & Country Life

"the Contrye life" whilst we launch Mary on her career as Maid of Honour to Queen Elizabeth. It was about 1595 that Mary Fytton, being seventeen years old, began her Court life.

Sir Edward Fytton, in his natural anxiety for his young daughter's welfare in her new and trying position, made interest on her behalf with a personage of importance at the Court, who was now Comptroller of the Household, and later on Treasurer.

This was an old friend of his own, Sir William Knollys, son of Sir Francis Knollys, and first cousin once removed to the Queen on her mother's side, through the Careys.

At this time he was upwards of fifty years old, and had been some time married to Dorothy, sister and co-heiress of John, 2nd Lord Braye, and widow of Edmund Brydges, Lord Chandos. She had been left her husband's sole executrix and possessor of much wealth for her life. In his will Lord Chandos grants her this life interest, "as his most faithful and loving wife, for her obedience, truth, and faithful love towards him."

Though Dorothy was a valuable prize as regards her wealth, she must have been considerably older than her second husband, and we have reason to believe he chafed at the chain that prevented his marriage with a younger and fairer spouse.

Sir William's brother, Henry Knollys, had married the only daughter and heiress of Sir Ambrose Cave, a first

first cousin of John Newdigate's mother, Martha Cave. Sir Ambrose was the courtly knight who picked up Queen Elizabeth's garter at a Court Ball, but when he offered it to the Maiden Queen "she would none of it," whereupon he bound it on his left arm and swore to wear it as long as he lived.

We have mentioned this Cave connection with both the Knollys and Newdigates to show that Sir William, who was an old friend of Sir Edward Fytton, had another claim to something more than mere acquaintance with his daughter Anne, through her husband's cousinship with his brother Henry's wife. Mary Fytton being just out of childhood may probably have been a new acquaintance.

The earliest letter we find from Sir William Knollys is addressed:

> To my verye lovyng frend Sr Edward Fytton Knight. [How it came into Anne's possession we cannot say.] Sr Edward I am sorye your disease shold so troble you, as yt depryves me off your companye whilst you remayne in London, but I will by no means that you troble yourselff w^{t}h going abroad, but synce you must undertake so great a jornye, be carfful to make yourselff strong until you goe. I wish I wear at libertye to accompanye you to Arbery & so to Drayton.*   I will

* His brother Henry Knollys' country place.

Court & Country Life

I will no ffayle to ffulffill you desyre in playing the Good Shepperd & will to my power deffend the innocent lamb ffrom the wolvyshe crueltye & fox-like subteltye of the tame bests off thys place, w^{c}h when they seme to take bread at a man's hand will byte beffore they bark, all theyr songs be Syrenlike, and theyr kisses after Judas ffasshion, but ffrom such beastes delyver me and my frends. I will w^{t}h my councill advyse your ffayre daughter, w^{t}h my true affection love hyr and w^{t}h my sword deffend hyr yff need be, hir inocency will deserve yt and hyr vertue will chaleng yt at my hands and I will be as carffull off hyr weldoing as yff I wear hyr true ffather.

Toching yourselff I will saye onlye this, that your love to me ys not unrequited & that whensoever eny occasion shall be offered wherin I maye stand you in stead I will never ffayle to use my uttermost power. In the meane tyme w^{t}h my best salutations to yourselff and my La : wishing you both health & happines

    I remayne ever
     Your assured lovyng ffrend
       W. KNOLLYS.

Thus Mary Fytton was launched on her Court life under powerful protection, but the "innocent lamb" soon turned out to be an arrant coquette, and Sir William's professions of fatherly affection rapidly grew warmer,

warmer, and blossomed into ardent love, which he confides in a series of letters to her sister Anne. Sometimes he veils his sentiments in the language of parable; but more often they are expressed in the frankest terms, apparently with no compunctions in regard to the existing Lady Knollys.

Mrs Newdigate (he writes), your kynd letter to your deere syster I have seene, wherein I fynd that though you be nearlye joyned by the law off nature, yeat are you more surlye united in the bond of love wch exceedeth all bands and bringeth wth yt in the end a blessyng where yt ys trulye contynued. Your thanks I accept as a recompence suffycient ffor my lynes, but your excuse off not presuming to write agayne I nothyng allow seming therby to make my white staff* an argument off your sloth yff I maye so saye, but to you & yours I desyre neyther to be head nor ffoote but in that equall proportion where frendshipp ys like to contynew surest & longest, & what ys deere to you ys deerest to me. Wherffore once agayne I will byd you the base hoping you will not allwayes kepe the gole in sylence. Some reasons mythinks might breede a better sympathye betwene us, ffor I ymagyne we both havyng to much Doe yeat want, though in dyvers respects our sumer ys turned

* The emblem of his post at Court.

turned to wynter, the one by the ayry element, the other by the earthlye.

The ffayrist fflowers off our gardens be blasted, yours in the budd by some unholsome easterly wynd, myne in the leaffe by the hoare ffrost and the dyfference ys that bycause the wynd maye change your hopes maye revyve & by reason off the contynuall ffrosts my lookyng ffor eny ffrute off my garden ys in vayne, unles the old tree be cut down & a new graff off a good kynd planted.

But I leave to parable and in playne englische wishe you what you most desyre. As ffor me my hopes being desperate & ffortune ever ffrowning, weare yt not that by the sonneshyne off some pleasyng thoughts I wear somwhat relyved I shold dye both in hope & hart. Yeat hope ys the onlye ffoode I lyve by & patience ys my pillow to rest uppon, both w^{c}h I wishe you to make your companions as remedyes agaynst all deseases off the mynd. Yf I have benne to long blame the matter w^{c}h leadeth me along, yff to bold w^{t}h you let my desyre to provoke you to a lyterall quarrell be my excuse, & yff to open empute yt to my trust. But yt ys tyme to leave trobling you eny longer & forgeattyng myselff. Wherffore wishing you all health & hapines both off bodye and mynd I desyre to be estemed in the number off your best ffrends, both ffor the love I beare to youre father

father & all hys & ffor your owne worthynesse remaynyng ever this 20th off Maye

Your assured ffrend
W. KNOLLYS.

It seems difficult to find any excuse for this writer's open avowal of impatience at the impediments that obstructed the desired end to his courtship of the attractive maid of honour. Neither is it easy to understand how Anne, the excellent Anne of whom nothing but good is known, could by her sympathy permit these frank avowals of Sir William's love for her sister. He even seemed so sure of her approval and co-operation as to ask for her prayers on his behalf in a subsequent letter. Here we find the disadvantage of a one-sided correspondence. There may have been extenuating circumstances of which we know nothing. Otherwise we can only be thankful we no longer live in the age of "good Queen Bess," but in the more outwardly decorous days of our Sovereign Lady Queen Victoria.

The letters which follow are given verbatim, for were they to be curtailed or any sentences omitted their historical interest and value would be injured.

They have been considered of sufficient importance to have been preserved for nearly 300 years in the Muniment Room at Arbury, though never yet made known even to the immediate members of the family.

It is also necessary to remember that letters of this period were written with infinite pains and much consideration, and consequently have a value far superior to the hasty scrawls of to-day. From their style and superscription they appear to have been invariably sent by hand, and months often intervened between their dates. We must now let Sir William continue the tale of his tantalising courtship. In his next letter he refers to Anne's hopes of becoming a mother, her previous expectations having been disappointed, as we may gather from his former remarks.

Honorable La: the more you goe about to disable your owne worthynes the more doe you make yt shyne in yourselff & by that means bring me ffarther endetted to so great a kyndnes. The least good thought of your well wyshing mynd ys a recompence suffycient ffor my smale power to afford you what you are worthye off, but such as they are comand and think that your Dearest Deare doth not wishe you better then I doe. As God hath blessed you w^{t}h encrease, so blessed be you ever & ffreed ffrom all dyscontents, & though myself can not but be now uppon the stage & playe hys part who ys cloyed w^{t}h to much & yeat readye to starve ffor hunger, My eyes see what I can not attayne to, my eares heare what I doe scant beleve, & my thoughtes are caryed w^{t}h contrarye conceipts, My hopes are myxt w^{t}h dispayre

dispayre & my desyres starved w'h expectation, but wear my enjoying assured, I could willinglye endure purgatorye ffor a season to purchase my heaven at the last. But the short warning, the distemperature off my head by reason off the toothake & your systers going to bed w'hout bydding me godnight will joyne in one to be a means that ffor this tyme I will onlye troble you w'h these ffew lynes skribled in hast, and wishing you all happynes a good delyverye off your burden, and your syster in the same case justiffyable, I leave you to Gods good protectyon, myself to your dearest systers true love & hyr to a constant resolution to love hym onlye who cannot but ever love hyr best & thus w'h my best salutations I will ever remayne

   Your most assured ffrend
  I would fayne saye brother
      W. KNOLLYS.

In the next letter he becomes still more outspoken.

Honorable syster, (I can not cheeose but call you so bycause I desyre nothing more than to have yt so) Your ffayre written letter & more ffayrlye endited I have receaved & read more then once or twyse seekyng to ffynd there wch so much you endevour to put me in hope off. Yt ys true that wynter's cold ys the murtherer off all good ffruts in wch clymat I dwell and doe accompt yt as a purgatorye allotted to me ffor my manye

manye offences comitted agaynst the Highest, the
rather bycause I am more observant & devoted unto
his creature then to hymselff, from w^{c}h to be delyvered
synce there ys no meanes but the devout prayers &
orasynes off my good ffrends let me entreate your
ffayre selffe to perce the heavens w^{t}h your earnest and
best prayers to the effecter & worker of all things for
my delyverye, & that once I maye be so happye as to
ffeele the pleasyng comffort off a delightfful sumer
w^{c}h I doubt not will yeald me the deserved frute off
my constant desyres w^{c}h as yeat no sooner budd by
the heat off the morning sonne but they are blasted
by an untymelye ffrost, so as in the midst off my
best comfforts I see nothing but dark despayre. I
could complayne off ffortune w^{c}h ledd me blyndlye
into this barren desert where I am readye to starve
ffor want off my desyred ffoode & off myselff that
would suffer my reason to be betrayed by my will
in ffollowyng so blynd a guide. But to all my
wounds I will applye your plaster w^{c}h ys patience, a
vertue I must needs conffesse, but havyng in a sort
lost hyr fforce bycause yt ys.fforced. Contynew, I
earnestlye entreate you, your prayer ffor my delyverye, and your best means ffor my obtayning that
w^{t}hout the w^{c}h I am not myselff, havyng allready
gyven my best part to one whose I am more then
myne owne. But I must crye scilence least I speak
to loude, comythyng this secrett onlye to your selff,

to whom as I wishe all happynes and your owne hart's desyre, so will I ever remayne

  Your most affectionat brother
    W. KNOWLESSE then I would.

Anne's first child, a daughter, was born in 1598. The godparents or "gossipps" chosen for the baby were Lady Fytton the grandmother, Anne's greatest friend Elizabeth Lady Grey, and Sir William Knollys. Immediately after this happy event Sir Edward Fytton writes as follows :

Good Nan, God in heaven bless thee and my daughter,* and contynew thy health and lyfe as my dearest friend and thereby comfort, next thy poore mother whose love and kindnes to me and her chyldren I ffere will shorten her dayes, but shee shall never waunt that comforte that I canne afforde her. . . . God blesse yor lytle one and grant thee as muche comfort I beseche him as ever mother had of child, but I ame sory that yor self will needs nurse her. . . . Thus longeing soare to see thee . . . faare well this xvii of May 1598.
    Thy treuest friend
      E^D ffYTON.

        And

---
* Common term for grand-daughter and god-daughter.

And again in another letter dated 3rd of July 1598 :

> Nan Newdigate, I ame to think my selfe muche beholdinge to you as a ffather cann be to a daughter. Yo^r mother will needs send ffrelan (?) and I send nobodye but my owne hart wch ever shalbe wth you where so ever my bodye is. I will se thee so sone as I canne and y^t is sone as I canne, and untill then I will love thee, and ever remeane mour thine then my owne.
>
> E^D ffYTON.

This latter date may have been that of the Christening, for Lady Fytton writes on the same day :

> My good Nan, I pray God bless you and my letle doughter. I longe to hear exceedinglye how you boeth do. I had sent befoer this but that I hoped sume other would have sent that do not. . . . I have sent you a nourse's rewarde x^{li} to by you a certle for my doughter. I wyll provid sume what when she is beegar to remember mee by. I longe to heer how all thinges abowte your new Charge goeth, for I parswaed myself that my sonne Newdygat wyll not go backe wth hys worde. I pray God send you well to doe wth it. And we can do you any good lett us know it and it shalbe don. If you heer any thynge of your sister I pray you let know, for I nevar harde ffrom herr synce. God blese you and yours

yours and send us all meri to meett. Gawsworth this third of July.

Your lovyng
mother A. ffYTTON.

Comende mee kyndly to your howsbande.
To my good doughter M^(rs)
Anne Newdygat at Erbery.

Anne seems to have been a special favourite with her great-uncle Francis Fytton, who had married the widowed Countess of Northumberland.
In a letter from him in this same year he says :

> Myne owne good neece, my earneste poore love unto you makethe me desyros to see you & especially in yor owne House, and yor kynde acceptance of my meanynge is soche as it byndethe me more to you for the same for wch I can but reste thankefull & so kepe it in my breste. And as my desyre to knowe of yor abidinge at home or not this winter was onlye y^t I ment to come to see you if possibly I might . . . but if I possibly maye I will see you this Christmas if not it shalbe moche agaynst my good will.
> Your Father's house in London this xi of November 1598.
> Your owne uncle & affectionat frend to all my powere
> FRANCYS FYTON.
I praye

I praye to be remembered to my cosen yo' Husband and to my younge mistress when she can understand my langwaige.

To myne especiall good neece Mrs Newdigate at hir house at Arbery in Warwyckshyre.

It will be observed that, even so early as this year 1598, Lady Fytton had cause for anxiety about her daughter Mary, who seems to have been more confidential with her sister than with her own mother.

Sir William Knollys accepts the post of "Gossipp" to Anne's little daughter in the next letter, and at the same time tenders advice on a subject that is not usually considered one of the duties of god-parents:

How desyrous I am in person to pfforme the offyce off a godfather myne owne hart knoweth & you shold have seene yff I wear w'hin myne owne power, but such ys my bondage to this place as I have neyther libertye to please my selff nor satisffye my good ffrends expectation, amonst wch I must accompt you in the fformost rank as well ffor your owne worthynes as ffor being so nerlye united both in nature & love to those wch I honor much & who maye more comand me than all the world besyds. But my thoughts off that partye I will leave to be discovered not by this base means off penne & paper but by my selff. Accept I praye you off my lawffull excuse

excuse ffor not coming my selff, assuryng you that I will be ever readye to pfforme eny frendlye deutye to you; I have entreated my brother Blunt* to supplye my place in makyng your lytle one a Christian soule & gyve yt what name yt shall please you. Imagyne what name I love best and that doe I nom'inate but reffer the choyse to your selff, and yff I might be as happye to be a ffather as a godffather, I would think myselff exceedyng rich, but that will never be untill one of your owne tribe be a partye player. I shold like nothing that you playe the nurse yff you wear my wyffe. I must conffesse yt argueth great love, but yt breedeth much troble to yourselff & yt would more greave you yff suckyng your owne milke yt should miscarye children being subject to manye casualtyes. But you maye tell me I am more curious in this poynt then I neede but I speak yt in ffrendlye councell not meaning eyther to contrarye your owne will or dysswade you ffrom your resolution yff by a reasonable perswasion your selff think not good to alter your pourpos. Thus w'hout ffarther complements wisshing you a happye mother off manye chyldren & your owne hart's
desyre

---

* Sir Christopher Blount, third husband of Lettice Knollys. Her first husband was Walter Devereux, Earl of Essex, and her second was Robert Dudley, Earl of Leicester.

desyre w'h my best salutations I comend you to God
& will ever remayne
Your assured poore ffrend & gossep
W. KNOLLYS.
To my verye Lovyng ffrend Mrs Anne Newdygate.

The suggestion of the writer in regard to the naming of his god-daughter was carried out. She was christened Mary; but Sir William's advice on a more domestic matter was not as effective. Anne was too devoted a mother to abandon any duty towards her child. Henceforth this correspondent always addresses her as his "Gossepp":

Fayre Gossepp the conveniencye of this bearer and the desyre I have not to be behynd w'h you in eny kyndnes ys cause that I maye not leave you unsaluted. The manye testymonyes you have made off your worthye respect off me bynd me to be thankfull by all the means I maye, and you shall ever be assured I will not ffayle to pfforme the part of a true ffrend whensoever you shall have cause to trye me. I am sorye I can not assure my coming to Arberye being under the comand off a greater power, but yff it be possible ffor me to break loose but a lytle I will God willing see Drayton and take Arberye in my waye. Untill then I recomend you to your best delights & thus wisshing you as much happines as your hart can think w'h my best salutations to your

your selff & my blessyng to your lytle one I remayne ever

Your verye assured ffrend
W. KNOLLYS.

Anne Newdigate had other correspondents at this time, one of them being Sir Fulke Greville (or Fowlke Grevyle as he signed his own name), father of the Sir Fulke Greville who afterwards became Lord Brooke. They were both men of whose friendship she might be justly proud. Camden says of the elder Sir Fulke, " he was a person no less esteemed for the sweetness of his temper than the dignity of his station. He was a gentleman full of affabilitye, which got the love of the whole countrie. For in his time no man did bear a greater sway in the countie of Warwicke." In addition to Sir Fulke's other merits he possessed the useful one of always dating his letters, but his handwriting is unusually difficult to decipher, partly owing to old age and partly to the gout, which often attacked his hand and arm. Occasionally he had to make use of an amanuensis, though always signing for himself.

Anne seems to have been much attached to him, and had given him the title of her "master," presumably from the love and admiration she felt towards him. The first letter we find from him is written in 1599, when he must have been about seventy-two years old.

Deere esteemed & best beloved servant All ye words in ye world cannot suffycyntly expresse ye Joy & comfort

comfort I take in bearying ye tytle & name off your
M^r. Many men are diversely affectted, some take
pryde off fayre howses some off theare welth some off
fayre wyffs & others off theare chyldrene; I only
glory y^t I have a servant wch conteynes all vertews &
ye same draws to her ye trew love & affecktion off all
good mynds & myne in good faythe sweete servant
in such sort that thoughe I have ye honor to be called
your M^r you have ye powre to comand me & any
thinge I have, & in y^t so redye to obey y^t I shalbe
most glad when you shalbe pleased to use y^t y^r awck-
tority: My servant farewell, be nott weery in well
thinckynge of him whose thoughts ar still bent to do
you honor. My syster Grevyle kyndly comends her
to you, & yff shee do nott love to speake whatt shee
thincks nott (wch I never yett knew her do) then shee
loveth you more then exceedyngly. Wee prattle
many tymes off you I wyshe your eares glow nott, I
desyre to be in all frendly sort remembered to
Mr Nudigate, whose felycyty I shall envy ye lesse, yff
he wyll accompany you once a year to this howse.
My brother salutes you even wth holl hart, I commend
my body sole lyff lands & goods into your hands, God
prosper you & yours so shall nott I fayle to do well.
From Beachampscourt this 20th off August 1599
   by him y^t loves & honors you
  Your M^r off your own favor & curtesye
      ffOWLKE GREVYLE.

The next letter, a year later, is written from Coventry, eight miles from Arbury, and is inscribed:

To my servant best beloved & deerest esteemed never to be changed M^{rs} An. Nudigate geive thes.

My good servant! I dare nott lett passe such a messenger w^{t}hout my lynes, lest y^t may be imputed to me w^{c}h I hate above all things, carelessnes or forgetfulnes off so faythfull a servant & so good a frend. I am nott yett so well y^t I dare adventure to ryde so farr: Butt when I feele myself able, I wyll vysyte you God wyllinge & in ye meene tyme & ever after love you & be redy to do you pleasure. To ye Lord I leave you & him hartely pray to geive you all things agreable to your noble hart.
From Coventre this 28 off Apreill 1600.
  Your M^r & ever assured frend
   w^{t}hout dissimulation
     ffowlke Grevyle.

There are portraits of Anne and Mary at Arbury which must have been taken about this date. The elder sister, attired in hoop, farthingale, ruff and distended sleeves, has the gentle, serious expression of her earlier portrait. She has the same dark hair and eyes, arched eyebrows and pale complexion. By her side on a table stands her little daughter encircled by the mother's arm. Mary Fytton is in full Court dress with high open ruff, large hoop and puffed sleeves. She must now have

have been at the height of her favour with her royal mistress. The unformed girl has developed into a high-bred-looking lady with handsome grey eyes, fair complexion, and rather a long thin nose. The portrait is only three-quarter length, but gives the impression of a tall slight figure. The expression has changed under the schooling of a Court life to one of almost studied demureness, leading one to suspect a vein of subtlety beneath; or is it because we know her history that we discern so much?

Amongst all Anne's numerous correspondents we only find one letter from her sister Mary. This is written in a scrawling hand, and contains nothing of interest, but we give it because it shows the affectionate terms existing between the two sisters:

> To my dearest syster M^{ris} An. Newdigate.
> Since distance bares me from so gret hapenes as I can seldom hear from you which when I do is so welcome, as I esteme nothing more worthie and for your love which I dout not of shal be equeled in ful mesuer, but lest my lines to tedius wear and time that limetes all thinges bares me of wordes which eles could never ses to tel howe dear you ar, and with what sele I desire your retourne, than can wish nothing then your harte's desir and wil ever continou Your afectionet sister
>
> > MARY PHYTTON.

CHAPTER II

Mary's Downfall & Disgrace

WE have now reached a period when stirring events took place at Elizabeth's Court in connection with one of our heroines.

Sir William Knollys at this time had other troubles to distract him in addition to his hapless love affair. He writes his next hurried letter when much disturbed by the disgrace of his nephew, the valiant but reckless Earl of Essex : *

> Fayre Gossepp, I must crave pardon ffor my so long scilence not growne by a negligent fforgeatfullnes off so good a ffrend, but fforced by a distraction I have had

* His mother was Lettice, daughter of Sir Francis Knollys.

Mary's Downfall & Disgrace

had concerning the Noble Erle off Essex wch hath made me carles to satisffye myselff or my ffrends. I leave to you to ymagyne the discomforts I take heroff when your syster ys ffayne to blame me ffor my melancolye & smale respect off hyr who when I am myselff ys the onlye comffort off my hart. She ys now well & hath not benne trobled wth the mother* off a long tyme, I would God I might as lawfullye make hyr a mother as you are, I would be near both at Arberye to shune the manye greiffs wch this place affordeth & she shold enioye the companye of the most lovyng & kynd syster that ever I knew. My hart ys so ffull off sorow at this tyme ffor my lo : off Essex being dangerouslye syck before hys restraynt as I am scant myselff. Receave therffore I praye you these ragged lynes from a broken head as a remembrance off (a) most ffaythffull ffrend who will ever be readye to doe all good offices wherein I maye stead you. Thus leavyng ffor this tyme abruptlye wth my best wishes off your best desyres, I comend you to God & will ever remayne

   Your assured lovyng gossepp & ffrend
           W. KNOLLYS.

God blesse my ffayre darghter & kisse yt I praye you kyndlye ffor mee.

No wonder Sir William was thus disturbed about his
                nephew

* Fits of hysteria.

nephew Essex. He was later one of the four members of the Privy Council sent to parley with him, when Essex, intoxicated by wild ambition, had assembled a crowd of his dependants with every sign of hostile intention at Essex House in the Strand. The other three were the Lord-Keeper Egerton, the Earl of Worcester, and Popham, Lord Chief Justice of England. After some parleying they retired with Essex into the house, when their graceless host bolted the door upon them in the inner apartments, whilst he went off to see what support he might hope for from the City of London. "Thus were these four of the Privy Council confined and left in custody of a rabble, in peril of their lives." In the end they were released by Sir Ferdinando Gorges, and Essex expiated his succession of treasonable attempts with his life.

In the next letter Mary Fytton appears still to be encouraging her elderly lover with hopes that she would be willing to wait for him until he was free to marry her.

> Fayre gossepp, your uncles sodayne depture and my cõming by chance cõming to London when he was readye to take hys jornye ys cause you must looke ffor no cõpleiments at this tyme, onlye you shall know that true affection ys as well expressed in ffew words as in manye, & I assure my selff your wisdome doth not measure love by lynes. So as havyng saluted

Mary's Downfall & Disgrace

saluted you w{t}h my best comendacions & assured you that I will be ever readye to pfforme toward you all the good offyces off a true ffrend: the best news I can send you ys that your syster ys in good health & going to the Court w{t}hin 2 or 3 dayes, though I think she could be better pleased to be w{t}h hyr best syster uppon some conditions. Hyr greatest feare ys that while the grasse groeth the horse maye starve, & she thinketh a byrd in the bushe ys worth 2 in the hand. But both she and I must have patience & that will bring peace at the last. Thus in some hast w{t}h my best salutations to your selff, and my kyndest blessyng to my darghter I wishe you your harts desyre & will remayne ever

    Your ffaythffull ffrend and gossepp
          W. KNOLLYS.

This is the last letter in which the writer and Mary seem to have been on the best of terms. A cloud intervenes which will be explained in due course:

Honorable gossep (writes Sir William), your ffew lynes but verye pythye and significant wear verye welcom to me & I think I shallbe fforced in as breiff maner to retorne you myne by reasons off this bearers hastye depture but w{t}h them a verye thankffull & brother-lyke acceptance off your kynd remembrance. Yt was agaynst my will I saw you not this somer I had pourposed yt but being restrayned off my libertye by necessarye

Mary's Downfall & Disgrace

necessarye state occasyons I was desposed off otherwayes. Yt ys true that wynters approch hyndered my jornye to Arberye and so unhappye I am as I never ffynd somer, but being ffayne to ffeede uppon the dead stork I lyve in doubt ever to enioye the sweete ffrute off my sommers harvest. My ground ys covered w^{c}h the bramble & the bryer w^{c}h untill yt be grubbed & cut upp ther ys no hope off good. Yt maye be you contrye wytts maye gyve councell in such a case. Advyse me I praye you in this extremitye, and yff I maye once bryng yt to a ffrutffull soyle, I doubt not but you shallbe ptaker off my longed ffor husbandrye. This bearer hasteth awaye & I will ffynd some other tyme to send to you, so as for this tyme wisshing you your harts desyre I remayne ever
Your most assured ffrend
W. KNOLLYS.

And again:

Fayre Gossepp havyng so convenient a messenger though my warning be but short I maye not suffer hym to passe by you w^{t}hout some salutations w^{c}h in regard off the humer I am put into though they can be but melancolye yeat to one to whom I have benne so much beholdynge as your ffayre selff I will ever be thankffull & iust. Mythinkes yt ys pytye that 2 bodyes & one mynd so ffirmlye united as your systers & yours shold not endure so much distance off place, but

but that you are both bound the one by hyr Maties servyce the other by a comandyng husband & yeat I that am at the next dore doe think my selff now ffarther ffrom the place I most desyre then in the begynning off my jornye. Such ys the varietye off this world & the uncertayntye off this tyme I must lyve in ffrost & snow subiect to blasts & all yll wynds & shall I ffeare never be so happye as to possesse the ffayre fflower off the sumers garden. I hope you dwell under a better clymate where the sonne somtymes comfforteth though the soyle be subiect to ffoggs & mists. Make a vertu off necessytye & synce your lott ffell not to dwell in the land of promes where all things wear gyven that wear desyred, work your owne cōtentment out off your owne worthines & be ever happier then your unffortunate gossepp who will ever be readye to doe you respectyble servyce remayning ever

   Your affectionate ffrend and gossepp
         W. KNOLLYS.

Anne's "unfortunate gossepp" seems to have been when at Court not only figuratively but literally next door to the abode of the maids of honour.

Sir Nicholas L'Estrange relates the following anecdote: "The Lord Knollys" (as he became at James I.'s coronation) "in Queen Elizabeth's time had its lodging at Court, where some of the Ladyes and Maydes

Mary's Downfall & Disgrace

Maydes of Honour us'd to friske and hey about in the next room, to his extreame disquiete a nights though he often warned them of it ; at last he getts one to bolt their own backe doore when they were all in one night at their revells, stripps off (to) his shirt, and so with a payre of spectacles on his nose and Aretine in his hand, comes marching in at a posterne doore of his owne chamber, reading very gravely, full upon the faces of them. Now let the reader judge what a sadd spectacle and pitiful fright these poor creatures endur'd for he fac'd them and often traverst the roome in this posture above an hour."

The next events in the Court life of Mary Fytton are chiefly taken from Mr. Thomas Tyler's work on Shakspeare's Sonnets,* to whom we are much indebted for his researches into the history of this Maid of Honour in order to make good his theory that she was the Dark Ladye of the Sonnets.

It may be as well to state at once we think this theory cannot be proved. From the portraits at Arbury, Mary was in no respect the brunette described by Shakspeare as follows :

> My mistress' eyes are nothing like the sun,
>   Coral is more red than her lips red :
> If snow be white, why then her breasts are dun ;
>   If hairs be wires, black wires grow on her head ;
>   I have

* David Nutt, 270 Strand, 1890.

Mary's Downfall & Disgrace

> I have seen roses damask'd red and white,
> But no such roses see I in her cheeks.

and again:

> Therefore my mistress' eyes are raven black,
> Her eyes so suited, and they mourners seem
> At such, who not born fair, no beauty lack,
> Slandering Creation with a false esteeme.

Mary, on the contrary, was fair, not "dun"-complexioned, her hair was brown, not "black wires," and her eyes were grey, not "raven-black."

Nor have we any hint in the letters that she had any personal acquaintance with Shakspeare.

Certainly, in the year 1600, William Kempe, the Clown in Shakspeare's Company, dedicated his "Nine daies wonder" to "Mistris Anne Fitton Mayde of Honour to most sacred Mayde Royal Queene Elizabeth." The name Anne is plainly a misnomer for Mary, and shows how slight was Kempe's knowledge of the "Mayde of Honour," though doubtless he selected her as his patroness not only on account of her natural gifts, but in order to ingratiate himself with one so high in favour with Queen Elizabeth.

The book gives an account of a journey which Kempe had performed morris-dancing from London to Norwich. In his dedication Kempe says:

> To shew my duety to your honourable selfe, whose fauours (among other bountifull friends) make me (dispight

Mary's Downfall & Disgrace

(dispight this sad world) judge my hert Corke and my heeles feathers, so that me thinkes I could fly to Rome (at least hop to Rome as the olde Prouverb is) with a Morter on my head. But in a word, your poore seruant offers the truth of his progresse and profit to your honourable view; receive it I beseache you, such as it is, rude and plaine; for I know your pure judgment lookes as soone to see beauty in a Blackamoore, or heare smooth speach from a Stammerer, as to finde any thing but blunt mirth in a Morrice dauncer, especially such a one as Will Kemp, that hath spent his life in mad Jigges and merry jestes.

To quote further from Mr. Tyler:

It was in June of this same year (1600) that there was a remarkable festivity at Blackfriars. William Herbert* was present as was also a lady with whom we shall be still further concerned in the sequel. The occasion of this festivity was the marriage of Lord Herbert (son of the Earl of Worcester) with a lady of the Court, Mrs Anne Russell. The Queen herself was there; and having come to Blackfriars by water, she was carried from the water side in a lectica borne by six knights. The bride was conducted to church by the nobleman with whom we are now

more

* The W. H. of the Sonnets?

Mary's Downfall & Disgrace

more particularly concerned, William Herbert (son of Lord Pembroke) and Lord Cobham. The Queen supped and passed the night at Lord Cobham's.

Rowland Whyte, in a letter to Sir Robert Sidney, dated 14th June 1600,* says:

> There is to be a memorable maske of eight ladies. They have a strange dawnce newly invented: their attire is this: each hath a skirt of cloth of silver, a rich waistcoat wrought with silkes & gold & silver, a mantell of carnacion taffeta cast under the arme, and their hair loose about their shoulders curiously knotted and interlaced. These are the Maskers: My Lady Doritye [Hastings], Mrs Fitton, Mrs Carey, Mrs Onslow, Mrs Southwell, Mrs Bes Russell, Mrs Darcy & my Lady Blanche Somersett. These eight dawnce to the musiq Apollo bringes, & there is a fine speach that makes mention of a ninth, much to her Honor & Praise.

And again, in another letter written shortly afterwards,† he says:

> After supper the maske came in, as I writ in my last; and delicate it was to see 8 ladies soe pretily and richly attired. Mrs Fitton leade, & after they had donne all their own ceremonies, these 8 ladys maskers

* "Sidney Papers," ii. 201. † Ibid. 203.

> maskers choose 8 ladies more to dawnce the measures. Mrs Fitton went to the Queen & woed her to dawnce; her Majestie asked what she was; "Affection," she said. "Affection!" said the Queen, "Affection is false." Yet her Majestie rose and dawnced; soe did my Lady Marques [of Winchester].

In the next January William Herbert became Earl of Pembroke on the death of his father. The goings on at the Court at this time seem to have been notorious:

> One Mrs Martin who dwelt at the Chopinge Knife near Ludgate tould me y^t she hath seene preists mary gentlewomen at the Courte, in that tyme when that Mrs Fytton was in great fauour, and one of her Majestie's maids of honour, and duringe the time y^t the Earle of Pembrooke fauord her she would put off her head tire and tucke upp her clothes and take a large white cloake and marche as though she had bene a man to meete the said Earle out of the Courte.*

It must have been about this time that Sir William Knollys writes to Anne in evident distress about Mary's conduct:

> Honorable gossepp so much have I benne ever beholdyng

---

* "State Papers," Dom. Add. vol. xxxiv.; cf. "Cal. State Papers," Dom. Add., 1580–1625, p. 411, where the name is erroneously given as "Lytton."

Mary's Downfall & Disgrace

beholdyng to you in your true respectyble good opinion off me as I shold greatlye blame my selff & be thought unworthye yff I shold suffer your letters to returne unanswered, not havyng other means to maniffest how much I accompt my selff endebted to you ffor your many kyndnesses, especiallye in your well wisshing to me in a matter wch most emported me, wch I think will be cleane extinguished though I leave nothing on my part to be donne ffor the contynuaince theroff. But synce I know this discourse will nothing please you, let me assure you that no ffrend you have shallbe more readye to doe all the good offyces of a true ffrend then my selff, wisshing the partye I spoke off beffore so worthye & ffayre a mynd as my gossepp hath. But synce wisshes can not prevayle I will hope the best & praye that God will recteffye yff enything be amisse, accompting my selff the unffortunate man alyke to ffynd that wch I had layed upp in my hart to be my comffort shold become my greatest discomffort. But whye doe I troble you wth these things, let me lyve in your good opinion & I will ever deserve yt, & thus wisshing you all contentment & your harts desyre I will ever remayne

Your ffaythffull ffrend
W. Knollys.

Mary Fytton seems to have been launched on a mad career

Mary's Downfall & Disgrace

career that could only end in disgrace. In a letter of January 26th of this year (1601) from Sir John Stanhope to Sir G. Carew we find this paragraph:

> Of the persecution [which] is like to befall the poor maid's chamber in Court, and of Fytton's afflictions, and lastly her commitment to my Lady Hawkyns, of the discouragement thereby of the rest, though it be now out of your element to think of, yet I doubt not but that some friend doth more particularly advertise you.*

Next month, on February 5, in the postscript of a letter written from the Court by Sir Robert Cecil to Sir George Carew, it is recorded:

> We have no news but that there is a misfortune befallen Mistress Fytton, for she is proved with child, and the Earl of Pembroke being examined confesseth a fact but utterly renounceth all marriage. I fear they will both dwell in the Tower awhile, for the Queene hath vowed to send them thither.†

Then we come to a letter (in the Record Office) from Tobie Matthew to Dudley Carleton on March 25 which contains the following passage:

> The Earle of Pembroke is committed to the Fleet: his cause is delivered of a boy who is dead.‡

Thus

* "Cal. State Papers, Carew MSS." 1601–1603, p. 13.
† Ibid. p. 20.   ‡ "Cal. State Papers," Dom. 1601–1603.

Mary's Downfall & Disgrace

Thus Mary Fytton's short but brilliant career at Court came to an untimely end in dire disgrace. The Maid of Honour especially favoured by the Queen and adored by the Comptroller of the Household only seems to have escaped imprisonment in the Tower by "commitment to my Lady Hawkyns" for her confinement.

It is not surprising that her parents were greatly distressed at this shameful catastrophe, though they still apparently hoped Pembroke could be induced to marry their daughter.

Sir Edward Fytton writes to Anne from London soon afterwards :

> Sweet Nan, I ame very sorrye that you are not well and so is your good Gossepe also [Sir Wm. Knollys?] who hath him comended to you hartylye. I pray you lett heer ffrom you as I doe, I ame in some hope of your Sister's enlargement shortly, but what wilbe the end with the Erle I cannot tell. So sone as [I] canne you shall heere, I have delyverid yor letter to my Lady Derbye* and so praying you yf this berer cannot otherwayse doe that you help to hyre him a horse to Lycheffild to my owst at the George : and so wth my very harty comendacyons I bid you farrewell this xxijth of Aprill 1601
>
>   Y^r loving father & friende
>   E^D ffYTTON.

* Second wife of Sir John Egerton, the Lord-Keeper.

Good

Mary's Downfall & Disgrace

> Good Nan mak sure that this berer have a horse to Lycheffild yf not to Chesshyre.

Her mother adds a few lines on the same sheet :

> My owen good Nan this letter must sarve for us boeth. bee waer how you take pheseck. let mee heer how you doo. Whan we heer any good newes you shall heer form mee. God blese you and yours
>
> Your lovyng carfull mother
>
> A. fFYTON.

There is a letter from Sir Edward Fytton to Sir R. Cecil in Lord Salisbury's collection on this matter. It is dated May 16, 1601, and shows that some pressure had been exercised to induce Lord Pembroke to consent to a marriage, but without effect:

> I can saye nothinge of the Erle but my daughter is confident in her chance before God and wisthethe my Lo. and she might but meet before in different senes. But for my self I expect no good from hyme that in all this tyme hathe not shewed any kindnes. I count my daughter as good a gentlewoman as my Lo : is though the dignity of honour (be greater onlye in him) w^{c}h hathe begiled her I ffeare, except my lo^s honesty bee the greater vertuoes.*

This letter is written from Stanner, where Sir Edward was obliged to stop on his road to Cheshire, his daughter being

---
* Tyler's "Shakspeare's Sonnets," ed. 1890, p. 90.

Mary's Downfall & Disgrace

being with him and too weak to travel farther. Thus he had obtained her " enlargement " from " my La: Hawkyns " keeping and was carrying her homewards, but apparently in secrecy.

Francis Fytton writes to his great-niece Anne Newdigate eight days later on the 24th of May 1601 :

> Myne owne sweete niece I thanke you moche for yor laste of the 14 of this instante (lately by me received) and so lykewyse for many other before, because I honor you and love you as any the deareste frinds you have. I suppose your father by his stolne jorne into Chesshy(re) (unknowne to me) hathe acquiented you w^{t}h somethinge concernynge yor Systers estate. Howe true I knowe not for I fynd haltinge w^{t}h me in theyr courses for her. God grante all be for the beste, but for ought I knowe & can see I see nothinge better nor cause of better hope then before & I wisshe all things for her good so well as you desyre w^{c}h is all I can doo, and so good neece fare well ten thousand tymes. ffrom my lodginge the signe of the Black Boye a Chandler's house neare the weste end of the Savoye in the Strand this 24th of Maye 1601.
> Your lovinge uncle and assured
poore frind   fRANCYS
fYTON.
> I praye you remember me very kindly to your good husband and doo longe to see you boathe.

The

Mary's Downfall & Disgrace

The next letter from Sir William Knollys must have been written after Mary had left the Court and gone to her faithful sister Anne. In spite of all that had occurred the infatuated man seems still a victim to her charms :

> Fayre Gossepp, sweete & pleasant was the blossom off my love, so comffortable & cordiall to my hart as I had therin placed all my delight, I must confesse the harvest was overlong expected yeat had I left nothing undonne in manuryng the same but that yt might have brought fforth both holsom & pleasyng ffrute. But the man off synne [Pembroke?] havyng in the night sowed tares emongst the good corne both the true husbandman was beguiled and the good ground abused. How much more unhappye am I who though w^{t}h all the care & industrye I can use to bring this soyle to hyr fformer goodnes, yeat ys yt ympossible ffor me to prevayle, & God knows I would reffuse no penance to redeme what ys lost. I write not this to greve hyr whom I have so much loved nor your good selff, ffor ther can be no greater punishment to me then to be a cause off eyther your sadnes to whom I wish so well w^{t}hout comparison. I know your syster ys to apt to be melancolye & you can apprehend hyr greiffs more deeplye then I wish. But you are not alone, neyther can eyther off you be so often remembred w^{t}h sad thoughts as I am ffor that w^{c}h I can not remedye & yeat can never cease to greve

Mary's Downfall & Disgrace

at. Be you yeat a comfforter & I will not be wantyng to add enything lying in my power to increase both your contentments, & yff you wear nearer that somtyme I might playe a part I wold not doubt but to paciffye though not thoroughlye to purge that humer off melancolye. Thus leavyng you both to Gods protection w^{t}h my best salutations & blessyng to my pretye darghter I remayne ever

Your assured ffrend
W. KNOLLYS.

Let me be I praye you kyndlye remembred to Mr Newdigate & the more yff he will come dwell at Brokenberyes.*

There are only two more of Sir William's letters to be given. The next refers to the proposed marriage of his niece Letitia Knollys, daughter and co-heiress of Henry Knollys and Margaret Cave, the latter being first cousin to John Newdigate's mother, Martha Cave:

Fayre gossepp havyng occasion to send this bearer to Drayton I shold ffayle in good manner & might iustlye be accompted ungratfull yff w^{t}h some ffew lynes I dyd not yeald you my best thanks ffor your manye kyndnesses w^{c}h I will ever be readye to requite to the uttermost of my power. Whether yeat you be delyvered or not off your pretye burden I know not, but

* Brakenbury, John Newdigate's property in Middlesex.

but in both I wish you as much joye & comffort as your selff can desyre. I praye you tell Mʳ Newdigate that hyr Maᵗʸᵉ understandyng off the match betwene Mʳ Pagett and my neyce doth so well like theroff as she doth not onlye comend hym but all those wᶜh wrought a delyverance off my Neyce ffrom hyr bondage, & yᵗ wear to long to wryte how exceedinglye she alloweth off the match. But he shall not need to speak to much heroff untill my Nephew Pagett hath benne here & ys desposed to publish yt. Whether your syster be wᵗh you or no I know not, but yff she be add somthyng to your love off hyr ffor my sake who would desyre nothing more off God then that she wear as capable off my love as I have ever meant yt, & what will become off yt God onlye knoweth. Let yt suffyce that my ffyrst love shall ever bynd me to love hyr, your selff and all that love hyr, & thus praying God to send you health & happines I remayne ever

    Your trulye affectionate gossepp
            W. Kɴᴏʟʟʏs.
Burne my letters yff you please.

We now come to Sir William Knollys' last letter and give it here, although the date is in advance of the period, to which we must return later. It could not have been written until after July 1603, as it is addressed " To my very lovyng ffrend & gossepp my
La :

Mary's Downfall & Disgrace

La: Newdigate;" and John Newdigate was not knighted until the above date.

Fayre & worthye Gossepp, your ffather being the messenger I maye not but aunswer both your lynes w‍ᵗh thys symple penne, & your kyndnes w‍ᵗh whatsoever a true honest hart maye afford, desyrous still to cherish all the branches off that roote into the wᶜh my unchangeable love was so ffyrmlye ingraffed. What yt was your selff & the world dyd know, but what yt ys my hart onlye ys sensible off, yeat maye I boldlye saye no earthlye creature ys Mʳˢ off my Love, nor ys like to be, as not willing to trust a woman w‍ᵗh that wᶜh was so treulye gyven & so undeservedlye reiected. Where to ffynd yt I know not, unles yt be eyther hydden in my selff or layed upp by some who suffer yt to rust in some out roome off theyr carles thoughts. But wear I not tyed to a white staff in court & had libertye I would like a knight adventurer never rest untill I ffound better entertaynment ffor so good a guest. But what spyritt guids my penne, or whyther doe I wander. You may guesse at my meaning, she ys not ffar ffrom you that maye dissipher thys rydle & I maye boldlye saye that Marye dyd not chewse the better part, yeat lett hyr I praye you know that no man can wish hyr more happines & contentment then I doe wᶜh I will be readye to maniffest uppon eny offered occasion, & though

though hyr com̃endacons to me in your last letter wear verye ordynarye yeat let me be remembered to you both in the best manner I can as one who can not seperatt hys thoughts ffrom the remembrance off former bands.

No more at thys tyme, but wishing you & my godsonne * health & happines I remayne ever

    Your ffaythffull ffrend & gossepp

          W. KNOLLYS.

Excuse me I praye you ffor not writyng to your unkynd syster whose so long scilence maketh me think she hath fforgotten me & herselff, I havyng deserved more than a ffew lynes, but I am pleased synce she will have it so.

In spite of this last touching appeal, Mary does not seem to have been inclined to respond to her old friend's protestations of affection.

Consequently, when in 1605 Dorothy Lady Knollys died, and Lord Knollys (as he was created at the coronation of James I.) became released from the ties he had borne so impatiently, it was not Mary Fytton who succeeded to the vacant place.

Two months after Lady Knollys' decease, her husband married Lady Elizabeth Howard, daughter of Thomas Earl of Suffolk, she being nineteen and her bridegroom sixty-one.

                We

* Probably Anne's second son, Richard, born in 1602.

Mary's Downfall & Disgrace

We may here briefly relate the remainder of Sir William's history as extracted from Burke's "Extinct and Dormant Peerages of Great Britain," 2nd Edition, 1840:

In 1614 Lord Knollys was appointed Master of the Wards, and within a short time installed Knight of the Garter. In 1616 he was created Viscount Wallingford, and advanced by King Charles I. in 1626 to the Earldom of Banbury. . . . He died in 1632 at the advanced age of eighty-eight. . . . The subsequent history of this peerage is one of the most curious in the whole record of peerage claims. Upon the decease of the Earl of Banbury, the inquisition found that he died without issue, but leaving a widow, Elizabeth, his last wife. His honours were then deemed extinct, and his estates passed to his collateral heirs, excepting such as he had devised to his widow, who remarried Lord Vaux. In a few years this lady produced two sons, born during her marriage with Lord Banbury, her first husband. They had at first been called Vaux, but now she set them up as the sons of the Earl of Banbury, and gave to the eldest the title of that earldom.

Litigation on this point ensued, with varying results for some generations, until 1813, when the claim to the Earldom of Banbury by the then representative of the family was finally rejected.

Thus Dorothy Knollys was avenged.

CHAPTER III

The Leveson Letters

WE here take up the thread of Anne Newdigate's life, which seems to have been chiefly spent at Arbury amid her increasing family.

In 1600 her eldest son was born and named John, the christian-name of the heads of the family for many generations. A second son arrived in 1602 and was christened Richard, probably after his godfather, Sir Richard Leveson of Trentham and Lilleshall, who was an admiral in the reign of Queen Elizabeth.

Sir Richard was related to Anne through the Fyttons. His grandmother, who was a sister of Francis Fytton, Anne's great-uncle, married Sir Richard Leveson. Their son

son, Sir Walter, was the father of our Sir Richard, who appears to have been born about 1569, and therefore was only five years older than his cousin Anne.

Richard Leveson entered the navy at an early age, and quickly distinguished himself in the various actions of the latter part of Queen Elizabeth's reign. His promotion was rapid. In 1596 he was knighted, and on James I.'s accession to the throne he was appointed lieutenant of the Admiralty of England, or Vice-Admiral of England for life. In the following year he was made Marshal in the embassage for the conclusion of peace between England and Spain.

When under twenty years of age he was married to Margaret, daughter of Lord Howard, afterwards Earl of Effingham. The marriage turned out unfortunately, Margaret's fate being a lunatic asylum.

There is a full-length portrait of Sir Richard in the drawing-room at Arbury. He is in a black dress suit with knee-breeches, carries a sword suspended from his side, and is standing by a table on which is a globe. In person he is tall and thin, with the complexion and eyes that accord with his red beard and moustache.

He was one of Anne Newdigate's correspondents, whose letters she has carefully preserved, and evidently these cousins were much attached to each other. His usual mode of addressing her is as "Sweet wyff," though at the same time he is on the best of terms with her husband, John Newdigate, whom he speaks of as "Jake"

The Leveson Letters

"Jake" or "Jak." It seems to have been in accordance with the fantastic fashion of the time to adopt terms of relationship between close friends which did not exist in reality. Anne has kept letters from women friends who address her as Deare Sister or Swete Sister, and were it not that we know she had only one real sister—Mary, the maid of honour—we should imagine she had been one of a large number of Fytton daughters. Among those who wrote to her in these terms are Elizabeth (Nevill) Lady Grey, Mildred (Cooke) Lady Maxey, and Elizabeth (Beaumont) Lady Ashburnham.

Sir Richard Leveson's letters are as frank and hearty as a sailor's should be. He never wanders into the language of parable, like Sir William Knollys, nor wastes pens and paper in elaborate compliments, as was too much the habit of the time. He seems to have been generous to a fault, always sending Anne presents and offering her the use of his purse. His letters have the advantage of being dated, with only two exceptions, the earliest of which must have been written before Sir John was knighted, being addressed:

To my Lovinge Cosin Mrs Anne Newdigate at Arbury, these with speed:
Deare partner I can wryte you no Nuse from this place because all Occurrants are According to the Time (semi mortua). They have resolved since my cominge up to send me out agayne, Though the principall

principall hope which drewe the Quene into this Adventure be alredy returned in to Spaygne.

I have delivered all the reasons and Arguments which my Littell experience can afford to disswade them, because I know that this Time of the yeare doth yeld so poore an expectation of proffit uppon that coast as I feare the voyadge will prove both fruitless and unfortunat.

But since the proiect is ther own the wholl course of the Jorney shalbe caried by ther own concells and Instruction from which I will not varye.

To be short I desire that the world should know how much I contest agaynst it, and therfor yf the successe be ill I do entreat my frendes (since I have no parte of the plott) to endevor by preoccupation to free me from the comon censure of men, which for the most parte is full of mallice and detraction.

Yf I could promyse but the least lyberty to myself I would once more come down to Arbery to byd you farwell : or yf you could be so happy as to be eased from the bondage of that pretty Nursery I would entreat you and my cosin Jake to meet me half way at the least. But since I see impossibillities in both I have purposly sent this messenger to kiss yor handes and to let you know that whersoever he be ether at sea or at land you have still power to comand

         RICHARD LEVESON.

London the 15th of Janu :

The 4th of feb. I am gone. Comend my service to yor sister and tell Mris Waspsnest* yt she bestowe [the rest is torn off].

Sir Fulke Greville writes to Anne about the same date, also complaining of the ties of her nursery and tendering advice on the subject of her maternal duties, which seem to have exercised the minds of more than one of her correspondents. But with Anne devotion to her children was her most prominent characteristic, and she never abandoned any of the rights of a mother towards her infants, as is her proud boast hereafter.

To his much honored best beloved and deerest esteemed servant Mrs An. Nudygate.

My fondlei beloved servant such as you left me styll I am, thoughe lame & uncertein in my lyms yett styll assured & constant in my love & frendship to you sorowynge in nothinge moore for you butt yt you wyll styll contynew a nurse & by yt meanes hold backe from such as much love & desyre your company : Ytt wyll besydes make age grow upon you & I wyshe you alweys greene & floryshinge as you wer when you were in your pryme. My pylgrimage groweth to an end being over almost to a full poynt off ye yeares yt kynge Davyd appoynts for ye yeares
off

* Sir Richard's nickname for little Mary Newdigate.

off a man wch is threescore and ten. I wyshe your yeares may be dubled wth such happynes & contentment off lyffe y^t you may be joyfully heare wth your frends & after have lyffe everlastynge, & in this godly humor I leave you to his blessed keepynge. From your chardge att my Lodge this 4th March 1602[3]. Your ever lovynge trew assured frend & M^r

ffOWLKE GREVYLE.

This letter, from the date, was written shortly before the death of Queen Elizabeth, which event, as we know, took place on the 24th of March 1603, and caused much excitement in the country.

Sir Fulke Greville took a decisive step when the tidings reached Warwick.

Camden tells us, " Upon the news of the death of Queen Elizabeth, he being at Warwick at the great assize came down from the bench and with some of his friends proclaimed King James which the judges of the circuit refused to doe."

Anne Newdigate, in her anxiety for news at this critical period, sends a messenger to London to her cousin Sir Richard Leveson, who writes to her in answer :

The bearer herof cominge to my Chamber befor I was up would needes have me to wright somthinge, therefor you are more beholden to his importunity than to

The Leveson Letters

to my disposition which at this Instant is ether very slepy or exceedinge sullen.

I am the worst Intelligencer in the world, for I never walke out of my way to learne newes, but what I know you shall have. The kynge is now at Newcastle uppon his way towards London, but we do not expect his Arryvall befor the funerall of ou^r late Quene which is appoynted to be uppon Thursday in Æster weeke, and about twenty dayes After we do looke for the Coronation. The Councell standeth as it did, but some Addition is resolved which is yet kept seecret: Southampton is at lyberty and promyseth much to himself: Monioye* I hope shalbe sent for and yor Sister's mistres uppon Sonday last did looke passinge merely [merrily?]. The Queenes old Maydes (or rather) the old Queene's Maydes (I hope) shalbe entertayned by the newe, in which nomber Nevill † by my consent shall weare the Admirall's flagge and his flagstaffe also.

Thus much for the Court, now to the Cittye.

Our

* Lord Montjoye was created Earl of Devonshire 21st July 1603.
† Mrs. Nevill was appointed Maid of Honour in 1601, and seems to have been a young lady of a lively disposition. She was not reappointed by the new queen. The ancient coat-of-arms of the Nevills contained a galley, and was sometimes called Nevill (Admiral), to distinguish it from the other coat-of-arms Nevill or FitzMaldred (of Raby), also used by the family. This may explain Sir Richard's joke about the Admiral's flag and flagstaff.

The Leveson Letters

Our merchantes with on voyce proclayme peace, then shall I and many other honest fellowes be layed up in the wardroppe. London streetes shall be hanged with Cloth of Gould when the kinge cometh, The Stones covered with Arras, the Cunditts runne Renissh wyne alredy, And my Lord Mayor uppon his Ass Ranketh his brethren in steed of a stand of pykes to receave the Kinge. Ether come up now and se this bravery or close yor eyes whillest you lyve, for I hope you shall never se it agayne, And let Jaks colpitts [Jack's coalpits] pay for all. Thus (deare partner) havinge opened my packe it resteth in yor power to make Choyse of the ware, You have it as I paye for it and yf my stuff prove good sweet partner let me have yor custome.

London the 12th of Ap^l 1603
Yos^r in all assurednes
RICHARD LEVESON.

Comend me to yor sister yf she be there, to lyttell waspsnest, Jacke and my godsonne, it may be I will see you shortly.

The reference in this letter to "your Sister's mistris" is difficult to explain, unless it refers to the so-called "mother" of the maids of honour at the time Mary was at Court. From the context one might have thought it referred to Lord Montjoye's wife; but at that time he was not lawfully married to Penelope, sister of the Earl of Essex and wife

The Leveson Letters

wife of Lord Rich. Charles Blount, 8th Baron Montjoye and afterwards Earl of Devonshire, had distinguished himself in the defeat of the Spanish Armada. The one blot on his career was his connection with Lady Rich (the Stella of Sir Philip Sidney), by whom he had several children and whom he married after her divorce in 1605. In a letter from Francis Fytton to his great-niece Anne we find there was some discussion as to whether she and her husband should come to London at this interesting moment. We cannot say if Anne were able to free herself from the " bondage of her pretty nursery " for the occasion, but her husband was knighted at Whitehall in July of this year, 1603.

In a postscript of Francis Fytton's letter he says : " I praye to be remembered very kindly to my neece, yor Sister " ; and on the next page he adds one or two items of gossip he had heard respecting the Queen's movements from one " Mr. Boold . . . as thoughe the Queene hathe had lately some myshapp (w^{c}h is not to be spoken) and doubted could not keepe the tyme apointed for her comynge." Consequently it was uncertain " when would be the tyme of coronacon if the facte be treue." He also mentions a probability of the " nexte terme " being " put off or at leaste not at london by reason of the greate concourse of people, the heate season of the yeare and feare of the sycknes."

Anne supplements this news with some of her own which she has written on the back of the same letter.

Mr Greville (she writes) haeth lost the secretoryship of Wales, it is given to a Scotsman my lo : Anderson. The queene is not delivered thoughe the report was so, onely shee was discontented y^t they in Scotland will not lett the young prince come with her : it is thoughte to be the lo : of Merle's devise for his staye. The K. was much trobled at it & haeth sent the duke into Scotland about the prince. The daye of crownation holdeth certaine. It is sayed from my lo : of hunt : boeth the K. & Q. come to Coventrye to corme* Sir Jo. H. & certainelye to Sir R. Spencer's,† wch is within 5 miles of daintrye, for so he tolde Mr Salter and doeth make provision, he haeth promised that I shall knowe the daye certaine of her comeing thither.

Before leaving this period of the accession of James I. to the throne we will quote a letter from Edward Reed, who seems to have been one of the gentlemen attached to Sir Fulke Greville's retinue, and who writes for him to Anne to give her the latest news of the time.

* Combe Abbey, near Coventry, a residence which Lady Harrington had brought by marriage to Sir John Harrington. Princess Elizabeth was sent by the Queen to Combe Abbey when she went herself to Althorp on 25th June 1603.
† Sir Robert Spencer was created Baron Spencer of Wormleighton 21st July 1603. The Queen and Prince Henry visited Althorp 25th June 1603.

The Leveson Letters

time. The letter is inscribed "to my much honored ladye the ladye Newdigate," and as it is dated the 14th of March must have been written in 1603-4. It runs as follows:

Maddam

Sr Foulke uppō his returne from Warwicke is much trubled with the gout in his hand and elbow, how it will increase or decrease I know not, but wish the best; his health.

The occurenses above you have (I assure myself) hard of, if not, there are great preparations for the sollem finishinge the cerremonise of the corronatione. As for the feast, the state thinks fit, it should be spared so great and unnessesarye expence, beinge needles.

Fower Earls are to be created, three of them are these, my lord Chaunsler,* my lord Treasurer,† my lord Cicile;‡ the fowerth I have not heard named;

Dewks

---

* Sir Thomas Egerton, Lord Keeper, was created Baron Ellesmere 21st July 1603, and appointed Lord Chancellor three days later; he was created Viscount Brackley 7th November 1616, and the Earldom which is said to have been promised to him was conferred upon his son, 27th May 1617.

† Sir Thomas Sackville, Lord Buckhurst, was reappointed Lord Treasurer for life 17th April 1603, and created Earl of Dorset 13th March 1603-4.

‡ Sir Robert Cecil was created Baron Cecil of Essendon 13th May 1603, Viscount Cranborne 20th August 1604, and Earl of Salisbury 4th May 1605.

The Leveson Letters

Dewks are so uncertayn I leave them untill they are assured; Lords very manye have expectatione: Havinge no way to manifest my respect to so worthy a frend but by fables I expect pardon for them, and remayne to my ever honored M^s youre ladishipe, Sr John, my pretty frend and yours

A servant
EDWARD REED.

Beachampscorte the 14th of March.

Sir Richard Leveson's next letter is undated, but being addressed to " My Lovinge Cosin the Lady Newdigate at Arbery," it must have been written after July 1603:

My deare sweet wyff though the comon reporte that flyeth betweene Arbery and London may geve me just cause of jelousie yet I will not looke bigge uppon you, howsoever you do uppon me, in hope to receave a good Account at my cominge home.
I thanke you sweet wyff for yor love to my sister pen* and although I fynde no abillity in myself to make a full requital yet I will entreat you to accepte this poore remēbrance as a Testimony of my Thankfulnes. And I pray you tell M^{rs} penellope that 2 or 3 wordes of her handwrytinge unto me some times will not weary the messenger nor discontent the receaver.

I have

* Mrs. Penelope Leveson or Luson seems to have been a great deal at Arbury.

I have now nothinge else to say but do entreat you as you love me to cõmand any thinge that is myne about Lillesell as freely as you do at Arbery. But because I have nothinge but wyld Chattell in a parke I may make you large promysse and of them make no dayntye but send to yo' Cosin Williã Meyor at all times that will obeye yo' warrant.

I intend God willinge to come down so soone as I have despatched on littel peece of a Buysines which I do howerly attend, and then you and yo' sister must shortly after prepare to visit my lodge. In the mean and ever

          I will rest
          faythfully yos:
               RICHARD LEVESON.

Before Sir Richard writes again Anne seems to have had cause to reproach him for negligence in his correspondence with her. The terms "husband" and "wyff" he makes use of read strangely to modern ears, more especially when cordial greetings are sent to the real husband and "our children."

Sweet wyff it is my fashion I must confess and my fault, yf it be a faulte to be less curious with thos I love than with others whom I less respect. If then my love and observance to you hath not bin so often tendered by Letters as my harte could afforde Let my promyse for Amendment and my open confession

The Leveson Letters

of my fault finde pardon for th' offence. On parte of yo' last letter sheweth some distrust in you of yo' husbandes love, which I should be very sorry for if I did not knowe that wher perfect love is setled there of necessity some sparkes of feare and jelousie must remayne.

But yf ever I be so unfortunat as to geve iust cause therof, which shall never be without just precedent motives : It shall not be don by signes & figures but in that fashion that doth best beseme an open honest frend.

Till that Time come, which I hope shall never come, be assured (sweet wyff) that I am and wilbe

  Yo' faythfull frende and lovynge cosin

        RICHARD LEVESON.

I have sent yo' Chayne though I have seen yo' own handwrytinge agaynst it : But no more of that yf you love me : I have sent also some garnetts, when you se the size yf you will send order to me how yo' stones shalbe sett I will do my best though I am badd at it and take it for a favour.

This 3rd of May 1604

Comend me to my fellow John and all ou' children.

On the 20th of October 1604 he writes :

 Sweet wyff yo' salutations sent unto me by S' Walter Leveson

The Leveson Letters

Leveson* are as welcome I assure you as they can be to any man Lyvinge and I thanke you very hartely for yor kinde remembrance. In these infected Times I know that you will wante many thinges which the Contrey will not yeald: And therfor good Nan lay any thinge uppon me that this place and my power can afforde and use no other body but my self. In the mean and ever I will pray for yor health and good deliverance and so rest

    Yo^r lovinge Cosin to his last hower
          RICHARD LEVESON.

Again on the 2nd Nov. 1604 :

Sweet Nan I have sente you by this bearer an odd Ruffe of a New fashion when yor Sister lefte it for you and wythall a poore Remnante of my own which I found in the Corner of a Trunke and do now entreat you to accepte in good parte. I longe to heare of yor safte delivery, which God in heaven graunte you. And whensoever my love or service may stand you in any steed : as I do now beare the Title of yor husband : so let me carry thus much credit with you that I wilbe more at yor Devotion than the best of husbandes are generally to the best reputed wyffes.
               And

---

* Probably his cousin Sir Walter Leveson of Ashmores, whom he mentions in his will. Sir Richard's father, Sir Walter, died in 1602.

And so sweet Nan with my eveninges and morninges prayer I comit you to the handes of the Almighty
Yo^r faythfull lovinge Cosin till death
RICHARD LEVESON.

In this month of November, Anne's second daughter and fourth child was born and named Lettice.
Two months later Sir Richard corresponds with her on a matter of some delicacy concerning the expected arrival of a royal infant, for which a nurse would be required of rank combined with other essential qualifications.
Anne Newdigate's claims for this post seem to have been warmly urged by her friends.

> Sweet wyff: in this shorte space of my Arrivall in these partes I understand not so much towchinge yor Affayres as I desire to know and therfor you must not looke for such satisfaction from me now as I hope to send you by my next.
> But fallinge aboard some of yor frendes neer Chancery Lane I have now brought them to be of ou^r syde albeit they were strongly agaynst us. (They do only take it to be my project and no other pryvat humor.) And we are all resolved to runne on Course (vizt to sound the pleasure of the great one how this great God send him us shalbe disposed) that thereby yo frendes may spedely resolve for you, ether to entertayne the proiect or to have the honor of refusinge it: in the meene Time yor own aptnes and sufficiency shalbe

shalbe so infused to the Q : as I dare assure you no other will leape over yor heade :

I mett yesterday with on of the K : phisitions my familiar frend and thinkinge to extract somethinge from him, by way of discourse at last he tould me that ther were divers Gentlewomens names put in to a Bill for this imployment and that the K : phisitions were to examine and geve ther opinions of ther aptnes for that Charge as by tastinge of ther Mylke etc.

This is probable but rather than my wyff shalbe drawen in by this kinde of election Ile walke on foote to Arbery to kepe her at home.

To be shorte I will use all my best faculties in handlinge of the buysines wherein Ile either Joyne reputation wyth hope of preferment or Ile do nothinge. But alredy I can assure you that you have had very good offices don for you which shalbe continued wyth my best helpe and so sweet Nan farwell

This 17th   Yos^r yos^r
of Jan : 1604 [5]   RICHARD LEVESON.

For want of paper I will wryte nothinge of Mr Marwood but you have bin too lyberall of my purse. Good Nan send my unckle busines letter away with speed.

There seems to have been a letter before this next one which was not sent :

Sweet wyff I wrote on Letter unto you 4 dayes sithence which

which hath stayed with me for want of a messenger :
Since which Time Ned Maynwaringe hath endevored
to enforme him self and as I thinke hath wrytten
unto you the substance of his Intelligence. I did
ever beleve that the old Lady had some pryvat endes:
albeit I will still pursue my end : vizt that you may
ether have it to some house of yor own with an
absolute power or ells sitt still and have the honour
of refusinge it. This messenger is in hast therfor I
say no more but desire to heare from you spedely so
in hast I rest

       Yos^r

      RICHARD LEVESON.

This 5th of fe : 1604 [5]
Comend me I pray you and excuse me to my fellow
John that I wryte not unto him.

The project falls through, and Sir Richard writes again on the 21st of Feb. 1604 [5]:

Sweet wyff since the wrytinge of my last it is
secretly tould me that a person of good quallety from
whos Alliance I have somtimes taken dependency
desireth the keepinge of the Child when it is borne
(and is like to have it y^t she seeks) and for the
avoydinge of all Competencye it is plotted that a
woman of some ordinary respect shalbe the Nurse
albeit ther be many sutors.

Thus much hath bin pryvatly delivered unto me and
by some casuall discourse I have found it to be
probable.

The Leveson Letters

probable. I dare not name the persons but you may coniecture whom they are. It resteth then for you wysely and spedely to resolve uppon knowledge wherof yor directions shalbe followed. And so with my love and harty wel wyshinge to all at Arbery I rest

Att yor disposition
RICHARD LEVESON.

The Q. is possest with so good an opinion of yor worth and sufficienty as wythin these 4 dayes she tooke occation to speake of you.

And now we come to Sir Richard's last letter on this subject, in which we find that Anne's old friend and gossip had also been interesting himself on her behalf:

Sweet wyff I can say no more unto you than I wrote unto you in my last which I hope is come unto yor handes : only my Ld Knowles hath promysed to wyrite unto you who discerninge the cariage of thinges desisteth now from ou^r former course but continueth still to you passinge well affected. It may therfor please you in yor next to me to bestow a fewe lynes uppon him Acknowledginge some thankes unto his Lo^{sp} and declaringe yor mynd to be as free from entertayninge unworthy conditions as you were apte at first to nouryshe any hope that mought bringe probabillity of Advancement to yor house and posterity which you are able to expresse in better wordes and I will

will deliver it yf you so thinke good with some Addition of my own.

And so sweet wyff nothinge doubtinge but yo' Acceptance of my love will equall any my profession and performance all shalbe as much tendered to you as can any

    And so I rest
        At yo' comandment
            RICHARD LEVESON.

This 8th of March 1604–5.

Thus ended this matter as far as Anne was concerned. The expected royal infant, about whom there had been so much intriguing, made its appearance shortly afterwards, but only lived two years. Little Princess Mary lies in Westminster Abbey, her small figure represented in full Court dress reclining on her elbow upon her altar-tomb.

A few months after the date of the last letter, in the August of 1605, Sir Richard Leveson died in the thirty-sixth year of his age.

This sad event seems to have been unexpected. Sir Fulke Greville (the younger), afterwards Lord Brooke, writes to Anne for information concerning it as follows:

    Maddam, I thanck you verie much for your kynd visitation when I was in these parts and will be verie glad by this messinger to understand of your good health

The Leveson Letters

health whom I send to that purpose, and w'hall to intreat you to acquaint mee what you heare of the maner of Sr Richard Leveson's death, and what report or opinion there is of his wealth, and how hee hath disposed of his estate : and in whom the trust thereof is specially left. This I desire to know for the love and honor I bare him whilst he lived ; And because therein your affection concurred w'h myne I must now respect and honor you so much the more : wherof I pray you rest assured. So w'h my verie hartie comendations to yourself Sr John Newdigate and to poore Penelope I rest

Your assured loving frend
ffULKE GREVYLL.

Good Maddam lett mee know what hee hath done for his sister Penelope.

We have a copy of Sir Richard Leveson's will, dated March 1605, made from the register now at Somerset House, from which the following extracts are taken :

In the name of the Almightie and eternall God Amen. I Richard Leveson of Lillieshall in the countye of Salop, knighte, being of pfecte health and memorye thanks be to God and nowe redie addressed to a iourney beyond the Seas in the service of my kinge and countrye, calling to minde the uncertaintie of all earthly things and that we hould and enioye our selves together with all our temporall blessings but

but as tenaunts at will to our good God that gave them, and consideringe the troubles that many tymes doe insue by the indisposition of mens estate I have theruppon in the tyme of health resolved to settle such things as I possesse . . . .

He then recites how he had bought up certain incumbrances on his own and his father's estate, and these he now dedicates for the purpose of carrying out the objects of a lease made between himself and Sir Edward Fytton, Sir Robert Harley, and John Tirrische. In this lease, which was dated two days before his will, provision was made for raising £10,000 for such purposes as he now appoints, viz. : Debts to be paid ; £100 a year to Edmund Manwaringe or John Tirrische as long as the foresaid lease continues :

Which saide some of one hundred poundes yearly during the continuaunce of the foresaide lease . . . . shalbe ymployed by them to such uses and purposes and such pson and psonnes as I shall appoint unto them by some private instructions from my selfe. Item I doe give lymitt and appointe one thousand pounds pcell of the foresaide some unto my welbeloved sister Penelope Leveson als Holborne. Item I doe give and appointe one thousand pounds to be paide unto Hughe Burnell in trust to the use and behooffe of such pson and psonnes as the saide Hughe Burnell standeth bound to pay the same unto by due

due obligacōn bearinge date this present mounthe of Marche which saide some of twoe thousand poundes to my saide syster and to the saide Hughe Burnell I desier may be paid with all convenient speede.

Then follow various legacies of £100 to £300 to friends, relatives, and servants, &c. &c. The residue of his estate hè leaves

To such pson * or psonnes to whom I have conveyed my lands nexte and ymediately after my decease by one paire of Indentures bearing date the three and twentieth of this instant Marche. . . . . And of this my last Will and Testament I doe ordaine constitute and make Sr Robert Harley, Sr John Leveson, John Tirrische and Samuel Bowdler my executors. In witness whereof I have hereunto subscribed my name and putte my scelle the xxvth daye of March in the third yeare of the reaigne of our Soveraigne Lord James by the grace of God kinge of England France and Ireland and of Scotland the xxxviijth

RICHARD LEVESON.

This will was proved on the 28th August 1605 by Sir Robert Harley, and by John Tirrische and Samuel Bowdler on the 6th of December 1605.

* This seems to have been Sir Richard Leveson, son of Sir John Leveson of Haling, or possibly Sir John himself.

CHAPTER IV

Widowhood

IT now behoves us to ascertain from the meagre information at hand how Mary Fytton had been conducting herself since her downfall and disgrace.

As far as the evidence of the letters goes she seems to have given no special anxiety to her family or her friends during this period, and to judge by the frequent salutations sent to her by Anne's correspondents, she must have been often at Arbury with her sister.

Good old Sir Fulke Greville, in a letter dated May 1603, sends his "comendations to your good syster." Sir Richard Leveson mentions her more than once in his letters

Widowhood

letters in the last chapter as likely to be at Arbury. Sir Edward Fytton, writing to his daughter Anne at a date we know by the superscription must be later than July 1603, says:

> Good Nan God blesse you and yor syster as my owne lyffe, peruse this inclosure and then send itt yor mother I pray you. . . . Yo^r best Gossepp & honorable frend [Lord Knollys ?] comendethe me to tell you he wyshethe you bothe as much hartes ease* as to hyme selfe & every day sayethe he shall not be well untill he see you bothe.

This letter is addressed

> To the Right Worshipfull the Lady Newdigatt att her house at Erbury nere Coventry.
> I pray you hand this at the bull in Coventry to be sent wth speede.

Having noted down these facts in favour of Mary Fytton, it is necessary to record that she is credited by Ormerod, author of the "History of Cheshire," with having had two illegitimate children by Sir Richard Leveson, Kt.

The authority for this scandal is "Sir P. L.'s MSS.," Sir P. L. being undoubtedly Sir Peter Leycester. But Ormerod

---

* The Heartsease or Pansy was the Fytton crest, and much used by the family as an ornament or device.

Widowhood

Ormerod is not accurate in his facts concerning Mary Fytton's later history. He gives her Captain Lougher as her first husband and William Polewhele as her second, when the reverse order should have been recorded.

Mr. Tyler tells us in his "Shakespeare's Sonnets" that Lord de Tabley, on the other hand, asserts that his ancestor, Sir Peter Leycester, in his MSS., gives the order of Mary's two husbands in their proper sequence, and that he further describes Mary's two children by Sir Richard Leveson as daughters. In any case this blot upon Sir Richard's memory rests only on the MSS. of Sir Peter Leycester. Whatever Mary Fytton may have been capable of, this particular scandal seems to be quite unsubstantiated, and, it is to be hoped, is untrue.

It should be borne in mind that Sir Richard Leveson died in August 1605. Up to a late date in 1603 there are constant allusions to Mary Fytton as her sister's guest at Arbury, and there is not a hint of any cause for anxiety or distress on her account, as is the case subsequently to 1605.

It hardly seems possible that so frank and genuine a man as Sir Richard Leveson apparently was could have been capable of writing the letters quoted in the last chapter to his cousin Anne Newdigate, addressing her as "Sweet Wyff" whilst carrying on an intrigue with her only sister. Nor is it likely that Anne would have preserved these letters as valued relics under such circumstances.

Again,

Widowhood

Again, the letter from Sir Fulke Greville (the younger), Sir Philip Sidney's friend, would hardly have been couched in the terms in which he writes to Anne for information respecting Sir Richard Leveson's death if there had been any truth in the record of so prolonged an intrigue. In Sir Richard's will, given in the last chapter, there is no mention of Mary Fytton by name, still less of any provision for her or her problematical children, unless she was to be the recipient of the £100 a year to be disposed of by private instructions.

It is to be hoped that Sir Peter Leycester was mistaken, though it must be acknowledged that Mary's after conduct may have given rise to humiliating scandals concerning her, whether true or not.

It seems probable that as long as Sir Edward Fytton lived Mary was outwardly decorous. He was evidently warmly attached to both his daughters, and Anne, at any rate, fully returned his affection. However, Sir Edward died early in 1606, a few months after Sir Richard Leveson, and it will be seen from two letters, written by Lady Fytton later that same year and early in 1607, that her daughter Mary was again in deep disgrace. Before quoting these letters there is one more to be given from good old Sir Fulke Greville, written by an amanuensis a short time before his death, which took place in 1606. Anne Newdigate seems to have had anxieties of her own at this time in regard to her husband's health, as we gather she was kept at home to nurse him. Even

Widowhood

Even when you see another's hand you maie judge in what state myne is, especiallie if the lines come from mee, and yett I cannot hope to have it better: My hart in all extreamities is alwaies the same & bent to shewe itselfe w^{t}h as true a spirrit as his that hath the trewest feelinge of all the sences y^t apptaine to man. Out of that right consideracion and yor owne worthie deservinge doe I bestowe this messenger w^{t}h thease lynes to see yo^u And shalbe much gladder to heare of yo^u & yo^{rs} beeinge well then I can make yo^u by anie nues I can give of myne owne abillittie, beeing sometyme troubled w^{t}h a stitch, sometyme the hart burninge, often w^{t}h a cold, but most w^{t}h an ill stomack wch maie as well come by seeinge your charge prosper no better : (as by anie store of Meate I eate :) and yeet yor fellowe & I have all the care wee maie to cherishe them. My comfort is as they prosper yor cominge is hastend wch I shall be glad of, As ever to doe anie office in mee y^t maie showe a kindnes to soe worthie a servant to whom w^{t}h yor deere little ons I commend my love & leave you & them to the blessed keepinge of th' Almightie.
From Beachampscourt Maye 26, 1606.
        Yo^r M^r of yor especiall favour
             and ever assured freind
                    ffowlke Grevyle.
I praie you I maie bee commended to Mr Whittall & Mrs Wood.

Widowhood

Sir Fulke died shortly after the date of this letter, aged eighty.

Lady Fytton (herself now a widow) alludes to his death in the letter we next give. It is addressed " to my best and dearest daughter the Ladie Newdygat at Erburie ":

My owen swette Nan I pray God to blese you and all yours. I am sori for the deth of good Sr Fowk Grevill your good ffrynd and mynde ; your loss is gret as can be of a ffrynd hee was a veri ould man, it was marvell hee lyved so long, not doubt but your housband and you shall ffynd his sone a veri honorable gentleman and won that wilbee glade of boeth your ffrynshepis. . . . Your brother doeth enter into phesick tomorrow ffor the payne in his nose God send it well Mr Neithsmyth doeth dout but cuer hym affoer Cressymas, if please God. I take no joye to heer of your sister nor of that boy. If it hade plesed God whan I did bear her that shee and I hade bine beried it hade saved mee ffrom a great delle of sorow and gryffe, and her ffrom sham and such shame as never hade Chesshyre woman, worse now than ever. Wrytt no mor to mee of her. Thanke my pritti Jacke for his token. I wyll wer it ffor his sack and sende hym another affoer it bee longe. Comend mee to Mall, Deck and lettle prete Letti. God blesse them all. Lett mee bee kyndly remembared to your housband. Prayng God to send us

Widowhood

us all well to meet I end, and wyll ever remayn to you A kynde mother.

A. ffYTON.

I would wysshe you to send to your sister this inclosed to see. I have left them unsealed you may reed them and scell them. Good Nan faell not. It standeth much.

Poor mother, what must she not have suffered to write as above about her erring daughter! Stern as she is in the first part, her mother's heart relents in the postscript, whilst Anne, as ever, seems tender and charitable towards this sister's frailty.

Notice should be taken of "the boy" referred to in this letter in connection with Mary's disgrace. In the following year she married a certain William Polwhele, about whom there seem to have been different opinions in the family. She is known to have had a son by him, and possibly this was the boy born before her marriage. This son was living in September 1609, the date of William Polwhele's will, and a daughter was born subsequently, who appears to have eventually married John Gatacre, of Gatacre in Shropshire.

Mr. C. G. O. Bridgeman, of the Chancery Bar, in his exhaustive and valuable researches when compiling a catalogue of the Arbury portraits, has ascertained that a Captain Polwhele served with Sir Richard Leveson in one of his expeditions in 1603, Sir Richard commanding the

the *Repulse* and Captain Polwhele the *Lyons Whelpe*. It is also worthy of note that the manor of Perton, in Staffordshire, the place where Polwhele and his wife resided, was the property of Sir Richard. May not a confusion have arisen from these facts, and was not Polwhele the one in fault rather than Sir R. Leveson? Lady Fytton's next letter gives her opinion of her new son-in-law, and must have been written in 1607, soon after the date of the marriage.

> My owen swett Nan I pray God to blese you and all yours. I wryt to you the last week that Mr Moer was a meen ffor the delyverie of your housbande's letter to my Lo: Chaunsler who gave it to his Secreteri and commandid hym that Chamberlen should answer it, wych I did not well lyke. Your brother came hether upon Wensday to see mee, and was to goe upon ffryday backe. I showed him your letter, and caused hym to go to Sr John Edgerton, hopyng hie would have doun hym ffavar in this or any other. What deck [Dick?]* haeth wrytten I know not, but this hee tould mee was his answer, that Sr John Newdygat wer beste to com and answere it hymselfe. It should seem sume other had aferme it —hie would not do your brother that kyndnes, as to send for the informacion gyven agaynst your housband
> that

* Anne's second brother, Richard Fytton.

that hie myght see it, but fell into rallyng agaynst you ffor speckyng agaynst the mareg of your sister to Powlwhyell—it was oute of your umar and that hie was worthee her. My ladi ffrancis * saed she was the vyles woman under the sone. To concleud they did use deck so unkynly as hie haeth no grat hart bournyng to go ther synce Cressynmas. I hade the kyndest messages from them that could bee and that they would com see mee. But Poullwhyll is a veri kave [knave?] and taketh the disgrace of his wyff and all her ffryndes to make the wordt [world?] thynk hym worthey of her and that she dessarved no bettar. It is longe to wrytt all I knowe, I would wyshe your housband to com hether. Gyve it owt I have sent ffor hym. Lett hym not dowt but to ffynde as good ffryndes as Chambarlyn. I shall have logyng for hym. Hie shall faer as I doo. Thus prayng God to defend us ffrom ower enymes and blese us, I end, remaynyng ever Your poure, kynde, greved
mother A. ffyton.
Pray your housband thynke no unkyndnes I did not wryt to hym.

If there had not been some previous scandal between Mary Fytton and Polwhele, why should her mother
thus

* Lady Frances Stanley, daughter of Ferdinando, Earl of Derby, and wife of Sir John Egerton, afterwards Earl of Bridgewater.

Widowhood

thus rail against the marriage? We infer that Anne too disapproved of her new brother-in-law. Probably it was not an alliance worthy of a Fytton, but under the circumstances one would imagine it ought to have been welcomed, though in silence.

Be that as it may, when once Mary Fytton became Mary Polwhele her family seem to have accepted the situation,* her great-uncle, Francis Fytton, even going so far as to approve of her husband as a nephew. He writes on Feb. 4, 1606–7, to Sir John :

> Good Sir John Newdigate, you are verie moche behoulding to my cosen Polwhele for his diligent care and frindley diligens in laboringe aboute your cause conteyned in the Lord Chaunsler's letter to you. . . .

And in his will, dated March 31, 1608, he makes a special bequest of his "usual ridinge sword" to his "nephewe Mr William Pollwheele whoe married with my neice Mistres Marie Fitton," and also bequeathed to him "the best horse," &c. &c., as a "remembrance & token of my love to him and to my said cozen his now wife," &c.

In this same will, in addition to some plate he bequeaths to Anne Newdigate, he makes the following bequest :

> Also I further will and bequeath to her my said neice the Lady Newdegate my bed being a bed of Downe, wch now standeth in my bed chamber at London

* See Appendix.

Widowhood

London wth a cannopie of yellow velvett & curtaynes of yellow double Taffitie & a yellow silk quilte to the same bed belonging, beinge such & the same as my selfe did usually use aboute my bed when I did lye & lodge their, beinge now in the house of Mr Thoms Shippe's Chandler neare to the Savoye in the Strand.

Probably this bedstead still exists at Arbury, and possibly the yellow "Taffitie" curtains also. The bed of "Downe" we trust has long been destroyed.

We quoted above a letter from Lady Fytton to her daughter Anne, in which she hoped that on Sir Fulke Greville's death "his sone wilbee glade of boeth your ffrynshepis." This was evidently the case, for Anne's cousin, Philip Mainwaringe, writing to her from the Court in February 1607-8, says:

Yo^r worthy frind S^r ffulke Grivell is ecsiding well whome I ame very much bound unto wch I doe impute to be for yor Ladiship's sake. If it please yo^u Madam when you next ritt to him to imploy me for the delivery of it I shall take it as a favor.

No wonder Philip Mainwaringe valued this privilege so highly. The life of Sir Fulke Greville (afterwards Lord Brooke) is a romance in itself. Camden says of him "he did so entirely devote himself to the study of real Virtue & Honour that the nobleness of his mind far exceeded that of his birth."

Widowhood

Lord Brooke never married, though, as Anthony à Wood tells us, " he lived and died a constant courtier of the Ladies."

After his death under tragical circumstances in 1628 (he having been mortally wounded by a servant who considered himself aggrieved), his body was embalmed and laid in the tomb he had had prepared in his lifetime. It is a handsome structure in black and white marble, occupying the whole of an eight-feet square building, said by Dugdale to have been originally intended for a chapter-house adjoining the Lady Chapel of St. Mary's, Warwick. Here, under a high marble canopy, rest the remains of Lord Brooke, whilst round the four sides of the flat tomb may be read the inscription composed by himself:

FULKE GREVILL
Servant to Queene Elizabeth
Concellor to King James
and frend to Sir Philip Sidney
Trophæum Peccati.

We must now return to Mary Fytton, whom we left safely consigned to the keeping of William Polwhele. This marriage only lasted until 1610, when she was left a widow with one son and one daughter.

We are indebted to Mr. Bridgeman's researches for the discovery of William Polwheele's will, dated September 19, 1609, and proved June 23, 1610.

Widowhood

He is described as "of Perton, Co. Stafford." His executors are his wife Mary Polwheele, Sir Walter Leveson, Knt., of Ashmores, and Sir Richard Titchborne, Knt., of Titchborne. The contents of the will are a devise of lands to his wife Mary until their son attains the age of twenty-one, then to his son William Polewheele: a devise of the parsonage of Brownsover als Rugby, Co. Warwick, one third to his wife, one third to his son William, and one third "to such child as my wife is now with child of," or failing such child, to his son William. The residuary legatee is his wife Mary.

The child expected at the date of this will was a daughter Mary, who afterwards married John Gatacre of Gatacre. Thus Mary Polwhele found herself again independent, though as a widow with two children.

Her sister Anne also lost her husband in this same year, 1610. Sir John Newdigate died early in the spring after a trying illness. His family at this time consisted of five children: two sons, John and Richard, and three daughters, Mary, Lettice, and Anne. The last was born in 1607.

When Sir John's illness took a serious turn in the latter part of 1609, Lady Newdigate's maternal love and anxiety induced her to frame a petition without loss of time to Lord Salisbury, Master of the Wards. The purport of this letter was to beg for the grant of the wardship of her eldest son Jack, a boy of nine or ten years old.

In

Widowhood

In those days these wardships appear to have been much sought after by persons even in the higher ranks of life, owing to the emoluments they carried with them. Anne therefore had no time to lose if she would keep the control of her boys' training and property in her own hands.

We find a draft copy of this petition of hers to the Master of the Wards, evidently composed by herself. It is labelled in the handwriting of her second son as follows:

> My mother's letter to my Lord Salusbury, Master of the Wards for my brother's Wardship when my father was sicke.

We give the petition in full:

> Right ho^{bl}
> Pardon this unmannerly presumption of a most unfortunate woeman though not unknowne and owte of memory wth yor Lo^{sp} yet as manie my nearyst frindes as my late father, S^{r} E^{d} ffytton my brother wth others too tediouse to nominate, having received sundery favors from yor Lo^{sp} (there meret none, myne much lesse;) yet being assured of yor owne noble hart's disposition and worthie compassion of all I am thereby incorraged (in this heavie extremitie being altogether frendles) to present my owne weaknes in all humble petition to yor noble censure. May it please

Widowhooa

please yo' honor that these scraling womanish lynes may bringe to yo' vewe this my humble sute. It hath pleased God to visit my husband S' John Newdigate wth sicknes so that the physitions stand in doubte of his recovery or to fall into a deepe melancholy : that you would bee pleased to bestow the wardship of my pore boye upon me, the unfortunate mother of 5 yonge children all nurssed upon my owne brests and nowe in burthen wth the sixt in this uncomfortable tyme. Ou' estate is smale, for when my father bestoed me in mariage all my husband's lands in Warwickshire were assured mee in Joynture wch was not above 200^l a yeare. The rest of his Lands lye in Middlesex caled Brakenbury wch are rayted to the uttermost and are nowe sett for 220^l a yeare, owte of which 40^l a yeare is estated to my second sonne ; the rest longe since convayed towards payment of debts and daughters' portions, having 3 : which cometh to a very great some for so smale an estate wch being separated, I and all my pore chylderen were utterly ruinated. Hoping to receave the wonted favorse yo' honorable clemency hath ever given testimonie of to widdowes and infants, And I shall be readie to yeald such gratuities eyther to my cosen phillip Manwaringe, or to some other as yo' Lordship shall apoynt : and I and myne bounde whilst wee breath to solicite the Almightie for yo' increase of honor to yo' owne noble hart's content. Ceasing to hinder yo' yor better imployed times, doe humbly take my leave & remain

   Yo^r Lordship's well wishing oratour
      A. N.

There are two parchments, both dated May 28, 1610, still existing in the Muniment Room at Arbury, granting Anne's petition as regards the wardship of her son and of his lands during his minority. Before, however, this satisfactory result was obtained, Anne seems to have had misgivings as to the success of her petition. We also gather it had been surmised that so comely and attractive a widow would be likely to marry again, and the mere suggestion of such a possibility seems to have roused Anne's keen indignation. We find another paper in her own beautiful handwriting, setting forth her doubts and fears, but to whom it was addressed we cannot tell.

In the meanwhile we should state poor Sir John Newdigate had died, which was doubtless a happy release, if the only alternative was his falling into "a deepe melancholy."

Anne's quaint paper runs as follows:

> What I have by my Lo: graunteing me the wardshipp if the marriage takeing from me the thirdes of my joynture being fond to the Kinge's use; & onelye one third parte of Brakenburye also fond to the Kinge; the other two parts to the Leasies, so that

that I shall fine to the Kinge & paye a yearlye rent dureing the minoritye of the ward : for the thirdes of my owne wch is absolutlye convayed me in joynture & shall loose so much out of my owne estate, wch I thinke was dearelye purchased for me, my father S^r Ed Fytton giving 120^l to my marriage ; keepinge my husband myselfe and a mayde & tow men 9 yeares of free will without ever haveing paye allowed ; my late uncle Mr Fras. Fytton undertakeing 900^l debts of my husband's 7 yeares since, out of his love to me, & payed them receaveing them againe to his owne purse but as Mr Newd : coulde convenientlye spare it to repaye him, of wch debt there is yet 200^l to be payed.

So that I loose my owne third part of Arberye to purchase a third owte of Brackenberye and must fine and paye rent for them boeth : and must be at charges for the findeing of the officises & what soever belongeth to the wardshipp, to be repaied when the ward is 21—if please him.

My Lo : honorablye graunted me boeth the wardshipp of the bodye and land, as in my letter was included as my sute to him. Therefore I wille holde it if his Los^p take it not from me ; & I make no doubte but his honor's hart is to honest to eate his owne worde : without my desert had urged him thereto.

What my Lo : shall fine me at or taxe me to paye I will

Widowhood

I will most willingly, but to loose this interest & right he so Noblye and freelye gave me: I never will whilest I breath. But to satisfy my Lo: if he be possected (by villanye of Mallice to me) of my brutishenesse to those deare Children that I have borne of my owne bodye and nurssed of my owne brests (theye never sucke other milke) thearfore I had neede to geve good example to them least they take of the mother,

I will enter into bonnds & toll of the worthyest frends & nearest kindsmen I have shall joine wth me, that if it shoulde please God to call me, or that I shoulde be soe accursed a woeman to marrye againe, that the wholl interest & comodityes boeth of the warde's marriage & the lease of the land from the kinge shall goe fullye & whollye first to the payement of my husbande's debts, his 3 daughters portions & other legacyes wch amount to but 100^l more, & a reasonable portion to be provided for this child I now goe with al that the father haeth not left a pennye: these thinges discharged whatsever the remainder is to my boye Jacke, being the warde. So that if I marye I will have estate in nothinge but my owne joynture dureing my lyfe: and if I lyve maister of my selfe methinges I deserve to be M^{ris} of my owne children whilest theye be children. This myselfe & friends wil be bound to performe to any of worthe my Lo: shall

Widowhood

shall nominate; but I scorne to be engaged to any base fellowe.

If a stranger had gott his wardship this had bin freelye gone, and then the ward when he had comen to full age shoulde have had al this to have light uppon him, wch summe in al is 3000′ 300′ & this childe I goe with not provided for. Where I havyng it am resolved to keepe them al and of my owne pore estate (else wil it never be raised out of ninscore pound a yeare unlesse he matche fortunatelye above his lineage deserves), & that I have from the kinge to goe yearly to these fornamed uses; which I thinke shewes a ill nature in me, and little affectionate love to my children; with a private purpose of my owne comoditye to defraude my children, for whose sakes onlye God spareth me in this world. For though the warde be my oldest sonne & dearest Childe, haveing but one sonne more, yett the rest are al of the same breede, & I thinke there is a conscience theye shoulde have what their father left them; wch were they not my owne, I being left his executrixe I should to the uttermost of my powers see faithfullye performed.

I shall marr my marriage by this meanes wch it seemes some report I much gape after. But since so manye deuils goe in shapes of men that my iudgement can not knowe the one for the other; God deliver me for ever being tyed to anye of them! For if I looke

Widowhood

looke for an honest man or a true frend, I must saye as one of the Roman Emperores did, I must goe to the graves for them, for theye are al dead & buryed.

Good, brave Anne! Though her sentences are involved, her meaning is clear as day. Whatever may have been the destination of this paper, and whether it went forward in these exact words or no, she appears to have triumphed in her object.
Her cousin Philip Mainwaringe, who had a post at Court, writes to her on this subject :

Good Madam, I am soery it was my ill fortune to be absent when I should have done you a frindly office, but yor Letter to my Lo: was soe passionate & moveinge as you did not neede any better meanes for the obtayninge yor desyer. Yet in my hearinge (my Lo: speakinge of Sr John's death & yor pittifull Letter) three or four great persons who I named to Mr Whytall* moved my Lo: very ernestly for yor good, who answered he had & would respect you. When Mr Whytall came to take leave wth me he tould me yor La^p had made choyse of me in yor Letter as yor kinsman who (if pleased my Lo :) you desyred should receve the benefit his L^p would appoynt

* Anne's faithful steward.

Widowhood

appoynt out of it wch kind respect I feare I shall never merritt but will infinitely acknowlege.

My Ladys Grace writ to my Lo : in the behalf of my Lo : Harrington & his Lady for the Wardship; His answeere was you had a grant of it alredy, & he was assured if her Grace did know the small vallue of it, she would not have writ for it. Therefore since my Lo : is assured of the meanness of it by yor own Letter you may doe me a favor if you please, to seacond that poynt in my behalf when you next write to my Lo : because you have more power over me then you can challenge of a stranger in whom you have no interest. Thus seasinge yor truble I ever rest

           to be disposed of by you

                    Ph : Mainwaringe.

Fro. Court this 26
of March 1609-[10].

CHAPTER V

Friendship

LL we know of Anne Newdigate's life as a widow only proves that she lived, as ever, first and foremost for her children. We also gather she was an excellent woman of business, and was admirably aided by her faithful servants William Henshaw and William Whitall.

Sir John Newdigate showed his implicit confidence in his wife's loyalty and capacity by leaving her the sole executrix of his will. After his death in 1610, when Anne made her own will, it was mainly a copy of her husband's, although as years went by she had occasion to make later additions to it.

Friendship

In 1614 she entered into an agreement on parchment with a sculptor, by name William White, to erect a monument in alabaster to her husband's memory in Harefield Church, where it may be seen to this day. Sir John kneels on one side of a desk clothed in armour, Lady Newdigate (also kneeling) on the other side, habited in flowing black robes with a coif and long veil. Below kneel their five children, the two sons facing one way and the three daughters the other. There is no record in baptismal or burial registers of a sixth child, although Anne makes so much capital out of its expected advent in her petition for the wardship of her eldest son. Probably it was stillborn at the time of her trouble.

The inscription on the monument is in both Latin and English. We here give the latter version :

> Here Wisdom's Jewell, Knighthood's Flower
> Cropt off in prime and youthful hower
> Religion, meekness, faithfull love
> Which any Hart might inly moove
> These ever liv'd in this Knight's brest
> Dead in his death with him doth rest
> So that the marble selfe doth weep
> To think on that which it doth keep
> > Weep then who ere this Stone doth see
> > Unless more hard than Stone thou bee.

We must now return to the early days of Anne's widowhood, and having recorded her indignant protest at the possibility of her being "soe accursed a woeman as

Friendship

as to marry again," it may be interesting to note what temptations she may have had to belie her own words.

We have a large budget of letters to her from a Francis Beaumont, a scholar and a gentleman, afterwards Master of the Charter-house, who was evidently an ardent admirer of hers and at the same time a warm advocate of the suit of another. This other is only known to us as " my cosyn Saunders."

Francis Beaumont was the second son of Nicholas Beaumont, of Cole Orton in Leicestershire, and of Anne, daughter of William Saunders, of Welford in Northamptonshire. His younger brother, Sir Thomas Beaumont (one of King James's numerous knights), married an heiress who brought him Stoughton Grange in Leicestershire. Sir Thomas also had a house at Bedworth in Warwickshire inherited from his father, and Francis Beaumont, who was unmarried, seems to have spent much time at one or other of his brother's houses. Bedworth, now a grimy mining town, is only three miles from Arbury, and well within easy reach for personal intercourse. It is difficult in these days to imagine where a house suitable for people of condition could have been situated.*

Francis

* There is an old house still called Saunders' Hall, which is very likely to have come to Sir Thomas Beaumont through his mother, and is the only dwelling at all probable to have been his residence at Bedworth.

Friendship

Francis Beaumont's letters are wordy and overflowing with compliments. They are written with great care in a very neat hand, and though he gives us the place whence he writes and the date of the month, he omits the year, so that it is often difficult to arrive at their exact period.

Anne Newdigate seems to have been in great favour with the whole Beaumont family, including the married daughters, one of whom was Lady Ashburnham and another Lady Dixie.

If we take the earliest letters as having been written about the time of Sir John's last illness, the writer must have then been nearly sixty years of age. Anne had evidently a due respect for his judgment, and consulted him when penning her " passionate and movinge " petition to Lord Salisbury, for there is a much reduced copy in his neat handwriting. We are, however, inclined to think she sent the one we gave in the last chapter, evidently her own composition, and labelled as such by her son Richard.

The following letter seems to have been one of the earliest from Francis Beaumont to Lady Newdigate, as he refers in the postscript to an invalid, who was probably her husband :.

> My best ladie and of all ladies that ever I knew myne onlie best and most noble Ladie, albeit I am at this present imployed in the behalfe of an olde servant of myne to commend a suitt of his unto my

Friendship

my Lo. of Southampton : yet not for any busines to any Lord or Ladie, or to all the Lordes or Ladies in the world, shall the least time overpasse mee wherein I may acknowledge the last dutie I owe unto my best and most worthy Ladie.

And now I appeale from all judgements unto the onelie judgement of my thrise-honored Ladie so discreete and so wise, whether she would not thinke mee most unthankfull, voide of all gentilitie, admiration and honestie, if for her last letter onely (though never had been precedent cause) I should not acknowledge my selfe most infinitelie bound unto hir for ever. But now I am occasioned for other haste to play Orlando, not Furioso, but di Lasso,* who sometime, when it is thought that he would ende his songe with some grave cadens and verie long note, doeth of a suddaine cut of all with a quaver or crotchet, his brevitie better expressing the patheticall conceite of the dittie than the longest musicall coardes he could devise to set downe. Thus wishing all healthe & happines to my best Ladie and all hers, I humblie take my leave and rest. Yours

most infinitelie bound and
readie to be commaunded

Bedworthe the viii of July.   FRANCIS BEAUMONT.

If

---

* Orlando di Lasso, the leading composer (next to Palestrina) of the 16th century. He died at Munich 1594.

Friendship

If Coventree could have affourded either pomgranates or Lemmons I had sent them unto my frend, but what I could get that I send, and my prayers for him to God, and my man to bring me worde how he is. I doubt not but he shall speedelie recover since God doeth make him a Patient under so kinde and wise a Physitian.

From another letter we quote a paragraph, because it refers to Anne's five children under the emblem of a sinkefoy (cinquefoil), an heraldic term for the pansy or heartsease, which was the Fytton crest:

Your faire & worthelie beloued Sinkefoy I most kindely salute, which being like unto a hartes-ease hath three leaves of one sorte and two of another. I pray God from my verie heart, that they may for ever bring ease of hart to that thrise-worthy Roote that bare them.

He is writing from Stoughton, and adds:

My brother, my Sister, my Neece Ashbornham & my Neece Beaumont desire y^t their loue may verie effectuallie be commended unto you.

In the next letter, written from Bedworth, he makes a request to his "Most honorable Ladie and worthy of mee above all Ladies to be honored," with endless apologies for his boldness, until he at length comes to the point.

Friendship

My suitt (good Madame) is that you wil please to bestowe upon mee as an insigne of your favoure, the copies of your two letters unto my Lo: Treasurer which you read unto mee in your closet. . . . . I protest unto your Ladis^{hp} by that dutifull love I owe you (for a better Sainte wil I not sweare by) that I wil in such sortt use them as you never shall have cause to reproove mee and as dearly esteeme them as a most rare juell of gould, etc. etc.

These letters were probably those given in the last chapter, as Lord Salisbury, Master of the Wards, was also Lord High Treasurer up to the time of his death in 1612. Anne has preserved a copy of her discreet answer:

Sir, I knowe noe faulte in you worthy of condemnation, therfore can not ajudge you. Mine owne imperfections I confess them manye; therfore my worth noe way challenging such admiration. For the coppye of those letters you desire, I must not denye them you. Yett I well knowe theye can be of no use to you: & the not so doine sending of them wilbe no prejudice,—for althoughe I shewed them to yor worthye selfe, it was the more to make him honored that made me so much bounde to him; that woulde so Nobly accept the pore weake & undiserett solicitation of An unfortunate Woeman his honoreable harte right censured. But how theye might

Friendship

might be if publishedd to the worlds eyes I knowe not. Excuse me till I next see you. For as you are pleased to respect me in an higher estimation then I have or can deserve; yett I hope never to geve just cause to make you repent that you grounded yor good opinion of her that is resolutlye determined to continewe.

Yo^r faithfull well wisheing frend

lett my love & best thanks I praye you be conveyed to yor al worthiest Brother & his good Lady.

Francis Beaumont, though so near as at Bedworth, sends an answer to this letter a day or two later, beginning, as usual, full of apologies, lest he should offend " my so noble and worthy a Ladie," and going on to say :

Where your Ladishippe writes that I missense your meaning touching the letters you read unto mee, because therein your purpose was but to show mee the honorable disposition of my Lord, I mistake the matter nothing at all. But let my good Ladie remember that I could not have discerned the graunt of that honorable Lord, without seeing ye thriseworthy request of my honorable Ladie, wherein I can commend no less the wisdome and maner in requesting, than your Ladishippe doeth the honoure and bountie in graunting : and therefore give mee leave (I pray you) as much to honoure my deare Ladie for the one

Friendship

as my good Ladie doeth honoure and thankfullie requite hir good Lord for the other. If you thinke that by wringing myne eye on the one syde I make things that be single seeme to be dubble, let mee alone (good Madame) with that which is myne owne, for myne imparcial judgement in this matter doeth direct mee with such a streight line as I knowe I can not be deceived.

In spite of this letter the writer adds as a postscript :

This day I purpose (God willing) to see my good Ladie, and so to take my leave, my brother & my sister determining the week folowing to goe into Lestarshire, and then to give hir the infinite thanks for those honorable courtesies, which never I can deserve nor requite during my life.
Bedworth ye 2 of Februarie.

In the interview thus foreshadowed, Francis Beaumont seems to have obtained the loan of the desired letters, or rather to have copied them from Anne's dictation. In returning them he writes as follows :

My best and of all most worthie to be my best Ladie, I was unquiet within myselfe untill such time as I had perfourmed your commandment and so have now sent you bothe your letters here inclosed. If they appeare not of such puritie and brightnes as they were when you delivered them, you must or blame or pardon the rustie

Friendship

rustie treasurie of my memorie from whense nothing is distiled that looseth not some of the luster it had when it was first infused. My ground worke had bene more sure if I durst have presumed to have borowed your copies : but I had no great minde to intreat them because I found in you so little minde to lend them ; yet as they are there is not (in myne opinion) anything amiss. Your owne they be and yours as much as your owne children be yours, in this onely different, that your children were borne of your bodie and these preatie inanimate creatures borne of your brayne : yet not still borne but borne stil to reproove poore mee. I utterlie discleame from any alteration in them, unles in some one or two places, I have added either if or and : which is an addition like unto two little pinnes, prickt into a faire and wel made vellet gowne, the same neither altering fashion nor substance; but yet peradventure making some one or two pleates sit more closelie then they did before.
That you so seriouslie and so often repent your sinne in giving me these two jewels (for no lesse doe I estime of them then of pretious jewels) God forgive you this trespass and I doe, wishing you would still loade mee with moe of these sinnes, until I also finde in myself some motion of repentance. You can not bestowe your favoures upon any the best freindes you have that shalbe more kindelie accepted then of mee, and your most loving freind my neece, who being a great

Friendship

great collector of monuments wil, I knowe, in hir booke of recordes reserve a prime station for my Ladie Nudigate's letters. And now mee thinkes, I may claime some indifferent good place (a litle before behynde the doore) in your frendshippe, by meanes of this new aliance with us, your la^{sp} being of late maried into my neeces sisterhoode.* Reprove me no more (most worthy Ladie) for making your letters too common : for had they bene the fairest and finest virgines in the world I could not have kept them more chastelie than I did. The first whereof I protest, from mee was neither seene nor heard of any creature living : the second indeed I have rehearsed, and I will tel you upon what first occasion I was moved. A knight (not unknowne to you) commended much a great Ladie (preferring hir above all others) for hir fayre wryting and most excellent inditing. When should I have spoken if now I had bene silent? I could upon this offer no less than compare my best Ladie with hir, who I knowe in these faire graces by many degrees did farre excel hir? For what should I have done (good Madame)? Either I must have bene muet and have layed my finger upon my lippes, or like a naturall foole have told [counted] twentie for want of other speache, or else

---

* The agreement between Lady Ashburnham and Lady Newdigate to call each other "sister."

Friendship

else have saied that, which I did say, which was as hott as a burning cole in my mouthe, before I had uttered it. After this my neece drawing me asyde (for good women take great pleasure in hearing other good women commended) intreated me verie earnestlie to bestowe of hir a coppie of one of your letters. It is enough (quoth I) that you heare one of them: a coppie whereof (as much as I love you) rather than you shall receive from mee, I wil cut out the tongue wherewith I utter it. What better observation of dutie towardes my best Ladie than this could I have used? But you say I praysed you. Therein I offended in deed, but the same was in the scant and not in the exceeding parte. O miserable world, wherein wel disposed mindes are rebuked for observing rowles of charitie, and for commending of vertue! Madame, my resolution is and never shalbe altered that my harte shall sooner be taught to leave panting then my tongue braught to leave praising where respectivelie I binde myselfe in any observant dutie. And here I could tel you a prettie tale of my cosyn Saunders, which I wil forbeare until I see you, and yet this much in the meantime to bring mee in better remembrance of the rest; he blames mee more for penurie than you doe for plentie, saying it is pittie that so worthy a subject should ever be praysed by such a barren and worthless tongue as this of myne. . . .

Friendship

No pardon I wil crave for the tediousnes of my letter, for I must have a pardon *ex officio*, because long tales and long letters belong to a comforter without limitation and most convenient it is I now use myne office to my dearest Ladie to make hir way seeme shorter, while shee is travailing thorowe ye wildernes. I pray God send you all the happines your owne heart can desire and as much good fortune to yor worthy children as he can wishe that loves them dearelie. So I humblie take my leave, etc. etc.

In this letter we find the first mention of "Cosyn Saunders," whose suit seems to linger on for a year or more. The only member of the Saunders family who would have been a likely aspirant to the hand of Anne at this time is Matthew Saunders, of Shankton in Leicestershire. He was the grandson of Francis Saunders, of Welford in Northamptonshire, and a great-nephew of Francis Beaumont's mother. He had married Margaret Skipwith, daughter of Henry Skipwith of Keythorp, but was left a widower in 1605 with five children. He was knighted in 1617, and died in 1623.

On the back of the last letter given above Anne has made a rough copy of the answer she sent this correspondent, in which a gleam of humour appears, where she alludes to that miscalled "barren tongue," if his speech were anything like as lengthy as his letters:

Friendship

These manye testimonyes [she writes] of the contineweance of yor frendlye respecte of me can not be by me so worthelesslye esteemed as silentlye to receave them, and neclect A little thanks (thoughe to pore A requitall for so rich A curtesie) and thereby also heape uppon myselfe that wch I hate to be burthened with all, haveing bin ever preciselye carefull rather to cherishe A good opinion conceaved of me then to give just cause to extinguishe it, knoweinge it much easiere to gett a frend then to keepe one. The adventure of the loosse of anye such in my record registred woulde be to me most troblesome. How precious the contrarye in my harts thoughts helde I leave to his judgement, whose barren tongue is seldome spareinge in discovereing his much more reverent conceate then deserved of yor assured well wishing frend.

A. N.

If this is a specimen of Anne's usual style of letters to her friends, one can only wonder if so involved and stilted a production found a place of honour in Lady Ashburnham's "booke of recordes," she being a great collector of "monuments." We confess we like Anne's compositions better when they come from her heart, and are both "passionate and moveing."
The next letter we give from Francis Beaumont omits both the date and the place whence he wrote:

Most noble and worthy Ladie I sent yesterday unto you

Friendship

you a blanke paper that your good La^{sp} might conceive thereby that I held my selfe so infinitelie bound unto you for your most excellent goodnes, as that out of my little wealthe of wordes I could not by any meanes offer that dutie for which most deservedlie I am indebtted unto you during my life. In which conceite of myne (if I did amisse for dutifull love is ever full of fearefull care) your owne preatie stoarie of the Canopy, and myne of Timantes* for covering affectiones wth curtaines may be my all sufficient warrant. Since which time I have read your little doubtfull mot, and wel understand what you meant by receaved, but what by deceaved I can not imagine. Unwarelie I see, I am faulne into a laberinth out of the which if my deare Ladie doe not direct mee, hee whome of hir gracious favoure she called hir comforter, was never him selfe in so much neede to be comforted, I pray God my best Ladie doe not take my no ill meaning in some evill parte. For I protest unto yor La^{sp} if there were but one droppe of bloudde in mee (were the same never so neare my harte) that would procure any undutifull thoughte against

---

* Timanthes lived about 400 B.C. He was a Greek painter of Sicyon. He is known mainly as the painter of the "Sacrifice of Iphigenia," in which Agamemnon conceals his uncontrollable grief by covering his head with his mantle.—The Century Cyclopedia of Names.

Friendship

against my so excellent & worthy a Ladie, I could never sleepe quietlie before I had let it out, etc. etc.

Then as a postscript :

The ingredience within your litle guilded pill is stil in my taste more bitter than any aloes.

It is a pleasant variation from these complimentary effusions when we come upon a little local news such as follows in another letter :

Your la^{ps} pleasure was that I should wryte unto you the occasion of my brother's so suddaine departure and speedie appearance upon commandment at the Courte. The matter was unknowne unto my brother him selfe and likewise unto Sr H. Hastinges and therefore may be conjectured, but can not truelie be reported by any other. The manner of their sending for was this. A letter was directed unto them bothe from the Counseile sent by a pourseuant, and commanding that they should without delay make their personall appearance at the Courte, there to understand the Kinge's farther pleasure concerning affaires pertaining unto him selfe. Whether the cause doe proceed from some complainte of the Greene chlothe touching provision (about the which this countrie hath bene often and for many yeares grievouslie trobled) or that the king please to imploy them in quenching the wilde combustion, that, flaming out of our two great houses, hath for this two yeares overheated

heated all Lestarshire (the one of these Gentlemen being an assured frend to the one house the other a neare kyndsman unto the other) or whether he meane to use their service touching this great sale everie where reported,—the truthe hereof no man knoweth, and in roving men doe more often misse than hit the marke. Yet of this I am assuredlie persuaded y^t it can be no matter of dangerous consequence unto them selves, being bothe as they are of such respective cariage.

Your honorable and worthy frend Sr John Gray* liveth: at whome though envie daylie barke, yet I hope, shee shall never have power to drawe one droppe of bloode from him. The same day I came from Arberrie he was at the Assizes at Lestar, where he was merrie and laught as men doe that are not dead.

Your most honourable and thriseworthy sister as faire as beautie it selfe, more fine and prettie than sparke of vellet and as wittie as Pallas, is, (and so I long wishe shee may be) in verie good healthe. Worthy shee is to be loved of that worthy Ladie that loves hir and shee that loves hir, as worthy to be loved as any Ladie in the world. Of these two sisters I have vowed never to speake without some of
their

---

* Sir John Grey, eldest son of Henry, Lord Grey of Groby, died *vitâ patris* in October 1611.

Friendship

their excellent and most worthy embeliments : so I thinke I doe now, and so wil I ever do hereafter. As occasion serves yor La^{sp} shall heare from me againe, being verie glad that by this opportunitie, a way is layed open unto mee to doe a dubble dutie unto my best and most honored Ladie, etc. etc.

The beginning of the last paragraph must, from the context, refer to Lady Grey, who always addressed Anne as " Deare Sister " in her letters, and not to Mary Polwhele, as might naturally be supposed.

Francis Beaumont fulfils his promise of writing again, and dates his letter this time from Bosworth (where he was a guest of his niece, Lady Dixie) "ye xx of March":

My last letter (most worthy Ladie) engaged mee in a bond of dutie to write unto you againe, if occasion were offered to any such purpose. My brother is now returned from the Courte, but so many thinges have happened concerning his journey, as may better serve for halfe a daies talke then to give but proporcionable matter to the contents of an ordinarie letter, And therefore I holde it best that these occurrences be not touched until I see my best Ladie, which should be (God willing) in these holiedaies, were I sure that my p̄sence might not become more troblesome then deserving to be welcome unto you. For I knowe about this time is your great preparation to offer your best and hyghest saccrifice unto your best

Friendship

best and hyghest Lord, wherein many desire rather privacie then to be conversant with companie : and I know not whether yor La^{sp} hath invited any frendes unto whome if my selfe be a stranger, though I be but one, yet may I be too many by one for such an appoyntment, having ever hated importunitie and inhumanitie as the two most extreme enemies unto civilitie.

Within fower daies after my last letter Sr John Gray was at Stoughton, where he spake much good of hir whome I most honour, for what can any man speake but good of goodnes it selfe?

Madame if you had been borne but under some fortunate Planet, it might have made you so wel beloved as you are, but that had then proceeded but from blinde fortune : but myne Ephemerides sayeth, that you were borne under a most blessed Planet, which makes you rightlie deserve to be loved of many, and that proceedes onely from vertue. Of this no more at this time, but never too much at any time.

My brother Thomas Beaumont is sicke, and I feare with some danger, my nearest kynsman is verie extreme sicke, one of my dearest frendes hath the plague in his house, and I am now going to visite another frend that lyeth in dying. When so many so neare and deare unto mee are so ill, I knowe and feele that I my selfe am not well. Pardon this letter, which is a monster, begotten by haste and brought

forthe

Friendship

forthe by greife, yet accompanied with the same dutiful affection that all the former have bene and subscribed as all the rest, etc. etc.

My nephew Dixe and my neece commend their best and most kindelie affected love unto yor good Ladishippe.

My many greifes (good Madame) doe move mee to make many suites unto God : in which I forget not to pray earnestlie for the healthe and happines of you, and yours, and shall receive no small comforte, if I know when I come to Bedworthe that you are all well, and for the same cause especiallie have sent myne owne man with this letter, that by him I may understand how you all are in this queasie* and sickly time.

* Sick with nausea. See Johnson's Dictionary, folio edition.

CHAPTER VI

Courtship

N the ensuing letters "my Cosyn Saunders'" suit is more openly advocated by his near kinsman Francis Beaumont, although the latter would seem to have been an ardent admirer of Anne Newdigate himself.

He writes from Stoughton on the 17th of January (probably about 1611 or 1612) as follows :

> Most noble and worthy Ladie, In my so often accesse and many letters unto your Ladishippe if either hereafter or at this time I commit any crime (for much speache is seldome without deserte of reproofe) I wil

Courtship

I wil first of all for them all entreate my good Ladie to pardon myne erroures, For desiring most earnestlie to have my Ladie Nudigate not onelie my good Ladie as shee is to all others, but myne onelie best Ladie above all others, I wil neither spare wordes nor workes, suite nor service, that may procure mee hir good opinion.

Ever since I last see your Ladishippe I have bene with my dying Pelicane* where I have wrought a miracle in somewhat reviving dead affectiones that lay buried for yeares seven foote within the earthe under a dead bodie.† Here I knowe my good Ladie can not well understand mee before shee see mee, and when I wryte I love sometime to leave behynde mee some obscuritie. For as in entertainment it argueth indiscretion to set all upon the table at the first course, and not to reserve something for the second: so in wryting to so wise and excellent a Ladie as your selfe, hee that leaveth not a handle in his former letter to take holde of in his next talke aymeth not right (mee thinkes) as he should at the marke hee shootes at. I wil set on a little more, and yet leave sufficient for a second and third course. I have contended with Mr. Haake in painting Phœnix and was not much inferior unto him even in

* "My Cosyn Saunders," as explained hereafter.
† May not this refer to Matthew Saunders' first wife, who died in 1605?

Courtship

in the same lineaments that by his running arte he endevored to expresse hir. And what if I should say that I thinke I did somewhat excell him? For he wrought but to the eye and I to the soule; he but painted upon a carde and I imprinted upon a harte; he set forthe but a dead beautie but I discovered a living beautie, and therewithall a mynde replenished with such vertues as can come under no skilfull hand to be descryved by a pensill. In this maner I have spoken of my Phœnix unto my Pelicane. Let not (most worthy Ladie) his labour hereafter become losse, nor his paines repentance; which must happen if the end hereafter prove as hapless as the beginning hitherto hath bene hopeless. Last of all, and then for this time I leave you. Absolve (most faire and deare Ladie) this letter from all suspicion of imposture, protesting unto you, that neither my tongue herein hath spoken nor my hand hath wrytten any thing, which my harte hath not ingenuouslie thought before. And so offering my service to be disposed by you I rest most readie
            at your commandment
                    FRANCIS BEAUMONT.

Salute I pray you in my name yor Sister whome the less I knowe and the more frendlie shee accepteth it, the more am I behoulding unto hir.

This is the first allusion we have to Mary Polwhele, who

Courtship

who appears to have been staying with her sister at Arbury, and was possibly an advocate for a second marriage to Lady Newdigate, she herself being on the point of making a fresh choice on her own account.

The next letter is written from what Francis Beaumont calls "a sicklie bodie," and is therefore doleful in its tone. He begins

> It is a comforte in great languishment
> To be bemoned with compassion kinde
> And mitigates the anguish of the minde.

Never was any rule so playnlie confirmed by example, as my Ladies most gratious and comfortable letter hathe approved this saying of the Poet to be true : wherein I see that noble spirite of hirs (which is hir second and worthieste selfe) possessing such varietie and copie of wit as can in most humilitie show greatest. . . .* Whyle in disabling hir selfe to comforte, shee hath proved unto mee that shee is the best comforter that ever comforted mee since I first breathed of aire. . . .

My neare kinsman that I lefte sicke was my cosyn Saunders in englische, in latine the dying Pelicane. I could wishe that in stead of this sicknes he had my Queene's evill, which is no less in her power to cure then to cause ; for the recoverie of that disease is

---

* Torn off by seal.

Courtship

is but to hang an Angel about the parties necke which must not be fastened with a ribbon, but with my Queenes owne armes, hir fingers being crossed one within another.

If wyshing were not the sustenance of fooles and that men of better wit might not finde some better foode to feede on, I could wyshe and wyshe againe. Discover not my little conception, for if you finde out this riddle, it may be that I shall have The Sphinxes punishment. I rather desire not to be understoode then to be reprehended. My yesterdaies sicknes stirred up all the humours in my bodie, and in my soule affection and honestie have appoynted a duel. Pardon mee now (my best and most excellent Ladie) or never pardon mee, or rather pardon mee now and ever pardon mee; for this letter standes in neede of a pardon of course, which being wrytten from a sicklie bodie, is like unto a sicke mannes dreame hanging together like lockes of woole upon a company of bramble briers. And so wishing that my best and dearest Ladie may never want such worthy comforte (when shee needes) as shee hath most bountifullie and honorablie bestowed upon my neede, or better wishing that shee may never be grieved, nor never neede any comforte at all, I commit hir unto his tuition, to whome I wil for ever pray for hir most blessed and happie estate. Bedworthe the xxii of marche, etc. etc.

Courtship

And then as a postscript:

> I would your Lad^{sp} did know how sodenlie and strangelie I was cured of my fit the last night, which was in such sorte as my Ladie never heard the like, nor any that dwells betwixt this and Antipodes.

The next letter has no date, but may well have followed the previous one:

> Most honorable and my ever best Ladie, not anything that came into my handes these many yeares was so welcome unto mee, as your good La^{ps} last letter. For having before more unadvisedlie than wiselie haszarded so worthy a Ladies favoure upon a mum chaunce, my diseased soule (after I had perceived myne errourc) could finde no reast until such time as your most comfortable electuarie was received. Many occasiones, I know, might have bene taken, which without vehement enforcing would of themselves have easelie faulne upon a harde construction: and then if my Queene had saied, the hares eares be hornes, hornes they must have bene: (what soever matter they had bene made of) and where had I bene placed, but amongst the number of the unfortunate beastes, that upon condemnation of life were dis‑charged?
> But I see such is y^t honorable and courteous disposi‑tion of myne excellent Ladie as will not suddenlie take

take exception against him that truelie honores hir, though occasion might seeme to be offered, and such hir most divine sympathising spirite, as can discerne intention, before almost it come into action, which opinion of myne, confirmed by that noble desert of hirs, if the same shall drawe mee into Palomon's* erroure, I will live and dye in heresie, and never revoke by recantation. . . . When you see my Counsailor, your onely sister, commend I pray you unto hir myne affectionate love, but not my quintessentiall, for that is becomme a confined recusant, having disavowed sacrifice unto all living temples, save onelie unto the living temple of the fairest and dearest deserving Cynthia.†

So craving pardon and wishing never to commit offense I rest

Yours most humble
to be commaunded
FRANCIS BEAUMONT.

I have sent unto my prettie Love my best blacke cocke, hatcht in a raven's neast, and desire yor good La^{sp} to speake for mee, y^t I may be hir best love until hir blacke cocke crowe and I wil desire it no longer.

To judge from the message to Mary Polwhele in this letter,

---

* *See* Dryden's "Palamon and Arcite."
† Another name for Diana, goddess of the moon.

Courtship

letter, the writer had made considerable advances in his acquaintance with her, and one is led to believe she was aiding him with her counsel in the matter of " Cosyn Saunders' " courtship.

In our next letter Francis Beaumont refers to an oration he had made before the King eight years previously, which shows us the date must be at least 1611, if not later, James I. having come to the throne in 1603. He writes from Stoughton on the 3rd of August :

> My service remembered to my best and most honored Ladie, I have sent unto yor good La^{sp} with this letter the oration that I made unto the King, which cannot of yor parte be so frendlie entertained as of myne it is willinglie offered, being though not the first, yet the first of my fruites that ever my best Ladie pleased to commaund. When it was alive and breathed by my breathe, it revived both fortune and favoure : fortune by alowance of the King : favoure by gratefull acceptance of the two noble men who intreated mee to perfourme that service. But honor it never had untill this present day. For though before it was fortuned and favoured, yet was it never honored, untill it came to be bounded betweene the honorable and thrise-happie handes of my most noble Ladie, more worthie to be honored than all the Ladies in the world. So now yor La^{sp} having it (as it were taken up againe out of the ground after eight yeares

Courtship

yeares buriall) if you shall suffer some skilfull crowner to revise the members thereof, there may happelie appeare a broken leg, a broken arme, or a broken necke, though at the first by advauntage of haste, it departed the world quietlie with a suspectles sepulture. My treasurie (good Madame) hath bene unroofte this twentie yeare, and so lying open upon winde and weather, whatsoever now comes out of it can not be otherwise than either mouldie or rustie. Such as it is, yours now it is, and myne once it was; you have commaunded and I have obeyed: and rather would I in this, or any other thing, loose the opinion of myne owne wit, than not yeald obedience to hir will, whome I honor so unfainedlie.

My cosyn Saunders commendes his service unto you, and tells me oft that I will loose your good favoure for fault of wryting: but I tell him that I will never loose it for any such fault, though wel it may be that I may loose it for fault in writing, my writing many times wanting wit, but never will to express the dutie I deservedlie owe to my so worthy and noble a Ladie. I assuer you and sweare unto you by my vowed service, that he loves you dearelie, and hath in him all the symptomes belonging to y^t languishing disease.

At the same time I was about this letter Sr George Belgrave comming to us to Stoughton to dinner, told mee, that my Ladie Gray, your sister, was brought to bed

Courtship

bed of a yong Sr John Gray, and reported unto mee withall (which was strange newes to my brother, my sister and to my selfe) that since our last coming out of Warwickshire your la^{sp} hath bene sicke of the mezels. Of your good recoverie I should be verie glad to heare; the testimonie whereof, if it were confirmed with your owne most worthy hand, would be unto mee a favour of treble value; which though often I have desired to see for more excellencie therein than you are desirous to heare, yet was I never so desirous as at this present, when it may witness unto mee that my best Ladie is as well as shee was, when I last left hir. I can but pray unto the all Bountifull Lord to send much safetie to you and yours; unto whose favorable protection committing you I humblie take my leave and rest, etc. etc.

Then follow the inevitable postscripts:

I must entreat your La^{sp} to pardon mee, though the number of my lines doe farre exceed the proporcion I allotted unto them, when I first began to wryte, ffor before I had sealed up this letter my sister Berkley* was come to Stoughton, who hearing that I was wryting unto you, intreated me verie earnestlie to commend hir love unto your kinde acceptance, and to make

* His sister Catherine married, 1st, Anthony Biron; and, 2ndly, Henry Berkeley.

Courtship

make knowne how glad shee would be of yor better acquaintance. When she comes into Warwickshire, she sayeth, shee will visite you : and if you come into Lestarshire, shee desires that shee may see you, and that you shalbe a most welcome guest unto hir.

About ten a clocke at the night came in yor sister Ashbornham, who hearing my La : Nudigate but once named, fell into such a discourse of love & kindenes, of kindenes and love, of courtesie and complement, of thing and thinges, as neither I can expresse nor this paper wel containe. At the last shee concluded that I must needes convey unto you with all titles of amitie a certaine conjuration, which shee sayeth can not be understoode till you two meete together. God help men, when such fayre ladies turne conjurors. I have sent the same unto you.

My nephew of Coleorton,* who promised mee the bucke in myne absence is gone into Lincomshire, where he meanes to tarrie this monthe, or he knowes not how long him selfe. Now am I going to catche him, who is wylder than any bucke in his parke. If I speed (as I hope I shall) I wil then discharge some little parte of the debt I owe unto my best Ladie,

---

* Sir Thomas Beaumont of Cole Orton, the head of the family, succeeded on the death of his father, Sir Henry, in 1607. He was created Viscount Beaumont and died in 1625.

Courtship

Ladie, to whome I am indebtted in all service I can for ever. And so I wishe you good rest, for now it is an hower past midnight bothe by the clocke and starres, and by my narroweyed scribling that write thus away.

As to the nature of the "conjuration" here said to be enclosed from Lady Ashburnham to Lady Newdigate we cannot tell, but it may have had something to do with "Cosyn Saunders'" wooing, as the "collector of monuments" was also an advocate on his behalf.
The following letter is from her, and tells its own tale:

Deare sister
Because pity is thought to be some ease in calamity & y^t I am so well assured of yor love & kinde respect towardes me, as I know you will bemoane me, I must needs send you worde how ill & painfull a Jorney I had after we parted, falling sicke in the midd way & had much adoe to get home, where I take (as I tolde you) small pleasure or contentment in this little solitary prison y^t I live in, but being here out of hope to injoye my frends presence I often please my fancie wth calling y^m to minde amongst the cheifest of whom yor selfe is never forgotten. And now out of mine owne greefes give me leave a little compationately to remember y^t honest kinde gentleman yor faithfull frend, & my kinsman, whose restles minde makes him

him more unhappy then eyther losse in his estate, or paine of body can doe, because it being y^t more excellent & sensable parte is of so much ye greater force to pplexe him, whilest his desire & affection (wch being satisfied are ye motives to bring him contentment) are in him continually tossed betweene ye rackets of hope & dispaire, who honoreth you so far as to acknowledg you worthy of much greater preferment in mariage then wth him selfe, yet being of councell wth his owne harte, he saith, none can love you more: his worth & meritt is better manifested daylie by him selfe & conceived by yor witty judgment, then can be expressed by me, though I thinke as much good of him as any frend he hath, doth. You need not think I am brybed, because I speake but sparingly of y^t you know to be his due; & yet I will not so far be led wth kinde regarde towardes him, as I forget my firme love to you, whose greatest happines & best content I wish as mine owne, but ye meanes I am not so well able to judge of as yor selfe & therefore will leave him & his future fortunes to yor good respect & consideration, comending my faithfull affection to yor well deserving selfe & so rest

Yo^r ever louing sister
ELIZA: ASHBORNHAM.

To my very worthy and much esteemed sister
    Y^e Lady Nudegate   d.d.

Courtship

We now give Francis Beaumont's two last letters, lengthy as they are, because they give us the curious admixture of his own ardent admiration for his "best Ladie" with an equally impassioned advocacy of his "Cosyn Saunders'" suit, which seems to have been finally rejected after a year's courtship :

My best Ladie,
I received of late a letter from my best beloved cosyn having before wrytten unto him with as forcible reasonnes as I could, to persuade him to desist from his endles laberinth and fruitles love, the conclusion whereof since (for ought I did see) could be but repentance, the continuance would be but the redoubling of greife, and to his former affliction the addition of a treble weight. His answere was that my too deare love unto him had procured in mee more impatience then he could alow of. For so farre was he from repentance, as that he preferred the acquaintance and least favoure of so noble and worthy a Ladie before the enjoying of the greatest Ladie in the world. When I read this I could not but bothe laughe and sighe ; laugh to see what a creature love can make of a wise man ; and sighe to see that my best and most honored Ladie had rejected this constant and more worthie man to make hir housband then (I protest) I knowe living. Alas poore lover, alas neglected servant, and

Courtship

and woe unto all men that at their first entrance into love esteeme women as Angels, but being overtaken with the wandering of their owne affectiones doe finde them in the end no better then merciless Tyrannes. My Ladie, I see, is not become like Pigmalion's Image, of a marble stone, a faire woman, but of a faire woman is turned into a marble stone. I can doe no more, I can say no more, but onely this, that I am heavie, sad and wearie; wearie of my life, wearie of my selfe, and wearie of whatsoever heretofore did most delight mee, but most wearie of all in thinking of my dearest, and worthiest, unfortunate Ladie whose wittes are farthest from home, when they should be readiest to doe hir the best service.

I see by his wryting to your daughter, and both wryting and sending to me, and not to you, that his suite is growen desperate: and therefore remaines no more of my parte but after making confession and taking leave to leave to folowe these wan hopes any longer.

My confession then (good Madame) is this, that never since I first breathed ayre, either did I or doe I honor or love any woman above your worthy selfe. But in my love are, and ever shalbe three sundrie sorted ranckes. The first is my naturall affection to myne owne generation: the second my passion of love to a woman, which is somewhat higher and hotter:

Courtship

hotter : the third the conjunction of my soule with the soule of another, which is the best and greatest, and this is and ever shalbe peculiare to your castaway, and to no other creature in the world. But yet if he had maried my deare Ladie, who hath the best parte of my harte, but least parte of my soule, then had my soule bene twined with both yours to make up Salomon's threefolded coard, that is so hardlie broken. But it must be as it may be, that can not be as I wishe it. My conceite of this triple love, of affection, passion & conjunction I discovered unto you long agoe in a letter wherein I wrytt (before you had ever seene my cosyn) that there had bene in my minde a duel betwixt love and honestie, yet honestie was and ever should be crowned with victorie, and the hottest love of myne towardes any woman when it came to feight with honestie, should have both his edge rebated and his poynt buttoned. So I sayed and so I wil say and thinke while I live, and am the better herein confirmed for that of late I have light upon Mr Spensers opinion so rightlie agreeing with that which nature had taught mee before, as the same might be thought to have bene drawne out of his discipline. And bicause I know how much you delight in all good learning, and in such honest verses, and to adde also some better tincture to my loath-to-departe, I wil set them downe as he wrytt them :

Courtship

    All naturall affection soone doth cesse
      And quenched is wth Cupides greater flame :
    But faithfull freindship doth them both suppresse
      And them with mayspring discipline doth tame
      Through thoughtes aspiring to eternall fame.
    For as the soule doth rule the earthly masse
      And all the service of the bodie frame :
    So love of soule doth love of bodie passe
      No less than perfect gold surmountes the meanest brasse.

So now (Madame) my soule I confess is his, so farre as one mannes soule may be another's, and foloweth after him to comforte his poore distressed and unpitied soule : my heart is yours, my dead heart, wrapped up in sorrowe, and buried in despaire, yet good enough to offer for a present to hir, whose harte is become so perseles and senseles as it hath lost understanding.

And seeing you have forsaken him, you shall with him also reject mee, who am whollie his for ever. And first I wil charme myne eies, that hereafter they never see you : myne understanding I wil so bewitche with strange illusions and fantomes, as it shall ever apprehend you as a spirite or a specter, newlie crept out of a grave, and then with frighting I will run from you as faste as my feete can beare mee ; my ever dying harte I wil cleave in peeces with continuall fretting to see hir an enemie to hir selfe who unto mee is so much endeared.

And hereafter you shall not neede to reprove my prayses

Courtship

prayses of you, nor to enquire the reasonnes wherefore I prayse you, for when you are commended by others I wil be silent, and byte my tongue betweene my teethe; and wil for ever hate all the virtues for your sake, that have made their cabine in the hard and senseles rocke of your harte.

And so fare you wel for ever my faire, deare, and unfortunate Ladie; not more deare then faire, but much more unfortunate then either faire or deare: and farewel your prettie and worthy children with all good blessinges from him that blesseth all: and farewel my good freindes, your honest and kinde householde: farewel Arberie my owne hoped heaven upon earthe, my now tormenting hell, and farewel with thee whatsoever thou shroudest from winde and wether; farewell my loath-to-departe and my selfe, for wee two wil goe seeke strange coastes together. And last of all farewel long letter, not too long bicause thou art my last: and when thou art gone from mee shew to my deare Ladie in what schoole thou wert brought up by these last woardes, which all theyr former fellowes caried with them.

   Your good Ld^{ps} most infinitelie bound
     and readie to be commaunded
       for ever
         Francis Beaumont.

In the postscripts that follow he becomes a little less lugubrious,

lugubrious, and in the last of them again refers to his
"counsaylor," *i.e.*, Anne's sister Mary, who in the
meanwhile has (apparently) married her second husband,
John Lougher, or "Captain" Lougher, as Sir Peter
Leycester calls him :

I received this weeke a letter from my Ladie Gray,
wherein shee wrytt unto mee that shee did hope that
hir suite for hir sister should have good success,
because in such matters I was verie fortunate. Thus
not onely faire Phillida but Philidaes faire sister also
doth flowte mee. And since I am flowted of all, fare
you wel all, for I am gone from you all for ever.
The last yeare I sent to my little Ladie Emelie* a black
cocke and much blacke fortune folowed : this yeare I
send hir a whyte cocke to see if change of colour wil
change fortune. I must entreat you when you see my
counsaylor to commend my hartiest love unto hir and
to tell hir that though shee be a maried wife, yet I wil
take leave to love hir for ever while I carrie within
mee a harte that can love. If hir housband wil give
mee this libertie (which is in myne owne power to
take

* He probably means Lady Newdigate's eldest daughter Mary, then
about thirteen years old. The allusion is no doubt to the Lady
Emilie, the heroine of the " Knight's Tale" in Chaucer's " Canterbury Tales," beloved by Palamon and Arcite. Chaucer's poem has
been reproduced by Dryden under the title of " Palamon and
Arcite."

Courtship

take my selfe) he shall love my wife (when I have hir) as much as pleaseth him, and for his kindnes I wil love him farre the better. Though I love not you, yet for your sake I love all your generation.

This long and piteous letter seems to have worked upon Lady Newdigate's feelings so far as to induce her to seek a personal interview with the writer at Bedworth. No sooner does she leave than he writes again what we take to be the last letter of the series:

My best ladie,
Presentlie after your departure from Bedworthe, my cosyn Saunders sent his footeman unto mee with a letter, the coppie whereof I send you here inclosed. It is beyond the limitation of my commission to impart unto you his secret meaning unto mee: but since everie freeman hath a wil, I wil also as wel as others sometimes use my freedome.
I perceive playnlie this matter is growen to an end, and that my long worke of subtraction hath bene but a drawing of nothing out of nothing, whereof ye remaine is nothing, save nothing, after more then a whole yeares wel-wishing unto you. If his most affectionate love towardes you, and your kinde love towardes him, and my bothe kinde and affectionate love towardes you bothe must end but with a shorte blacke crotchet, as Orlando di Lasso closed up (it perisheth) when I have sayed but this (I am for ever sorye)

Courtship

sorye) then I have done. After many troubles y' have chaunced bothe to my cosyn and mee in prosecution of this desire, our hope was, that God would in the end turne our mourninges to mirthe, unloose our sackes, and girde us with gladnes, which had come to pass if this had happened, and that our hope of Cynthines conjunction had not proved a wry aspect of a sextile.

What I could I have done and all that I have done proceeded of a most sincere love unto you bothe. Yet I must confess that in my laboures I did not a little respect my selfe, when I thought, by entercourse with two such excellent and worthy frendes, that Arberie should have bene my little heaven upon earthe, where all my misfortunes, my melancholie passiones, and heapes of greife should have found their present remedies. But like as Troylus once sayed, so I say:

> All this I did, and I can doe no more;
> She cruel is and woe is mee therefore.

This is the last time that ever I wil move you in this or any matter to like purpose, taking my leave of this suite as my cosyn hath done of Warwickshire in his former letter unto mee. Yet never wil I forget that I have obtained the frendshippe of a most noble Ladie, which I ever hope to holde though my cosyn have miste the accomplishment of his desired love.

And

Courtship

And so wishing continuallie to possess the same by whatsoever service I can devise, I take my leave and rest

    Your good Lad^{ps} most infinitelie
    bound and readie to be commaunded
          FRANCIS BEAUMONT.

My brother my sister my neece with all the best of this societie salute you in moe kind wordes then a sheete of paper can containe.

If it please you, the sworde may be sent by this bearer my cosyn Saunders boy.

The occasion of my cosyn Saunders letter unto mee whereof I have sent you the Coppie was this. Upon Mounday his man coming to Bedworthe with my Ladie Grayes letter I sent him all that night with a letter of myne to his master to have had him to have met you at Bedworthe upon Tewsday.

But you see his love is dying, not as vertuous soules departe in myldnes, or as men leave this world after a consumption, but with such desperate panges as are much more to be pitied by many degrees then I thinke they are. Of mee I knowe they are pitied even with my soule's greife: of you I knowe not how, you know best for I know nothing y^t lyeth hid in other hartes.

In this sad fashion exit "Cosyn Saunders" from the life-story of our heroines. We hear no more of him, but if our

Courtship

our supposition is right, and he was Matthew Saunders, of Shankton in Leicestershire, about this date he consoled himself by erecting an elaborate monument to the memory of his first wife, Margaret Skipwith, although her death took place in 1605, seven or eight years before his final dismissal as a wooer of Lady Newdigate. Neither has Anne preserved any later letters from Francis Beaumont. The latter may still have been a neighbour occasionally, although his brother and host, Sir Thomas Beaumont, died in 1612. It was five years later, in 1617, that Francis Beaumont was appointed (fourth) Master of the Charterhouse. He died in 1624, and is buried in the chapel. On his monument an effigy of him may be seen kneeling at a desk.

It may be interesting to students to know that he it was who, in 1597, addressed to " his very loving friend Mr Thomas Speght," a "judicious apology for the supposed levities of Chaucer" prefixed to the 1598 edition of Chaucer's works, and erroneously attributed to Francis Beaumont the poet (then only thirteen years old).

Anne Lytton
Lady Newdigate

CHAPTER VII

The Valley of Death

NE of Anne Newdigate's chief friends was Elizabeth, daughter of Edward Nevill, Lord Abergavenny, and wife of Sir John Grey, eldest son of Lord Grey of Groby. In Francis Beaumont's letters she is frequently mentioned as a friend and near neighbour in Leicestershire. There are a number of letters from Lady Grey to her "Deerst Sister" Anne Newdigate in the Muniment Room at Arbury, but are chiefly about her own concerns. She became a widow in October 1611, and then seems to have had some trouble with her father-in-law, Lord Grey of Groby, about money matters, her husband having died involved in debt.

The Valley of Death

Anne proved herself a sympathetic and useful ally in her friend's difficulties, and she has preserved the draft of a letter from herself to Lady Graye about this period which is so prettily expressed that it is given here as an example of her happier style:

> My harts al honoring La: I did forbeare to send these wch misfortune cast into my custody till so fitt an opertunity gave me cause to present them on to you: These are al that came to my hands but only one deede wch my weake opinion tells me is as well with helde since as safe in my keepinge as my love to your worthy self is assured. Al the actions of my pore lives pilgermages performance (of use to you) is to solicite our merciful redimer to whom I daily offer my sincere prayers that he would be pleased to power uppon you as many blessed comforts as in his rich goodness he vouchsafeth to bestowe uppon his best beloved. Wth the presentation of my service to your deare selfe do humbly take my leave, And must cease to live before I can cease to be
>
> faithfully yours
A. N.

Lady Grey's answer is as follows:

> Deare Sister I have receaved by My worthy frinde Mr Sanders all those thinges which your love haith so carfully kepte for mee: for the deede you have don

don mee a great favor to retaine it for it wolde be dangrus for mee to have it till busnises are better setled betweene my lord and my frinds for the good of my childrin. I only desir a coppye of it by the first opertunity that I may shewe it councell to knowe of whatt strangth it will be to tye my lord Gray: my ieys will not give me leve to say more of this or of any other busnis so I leve it to this worthy berer that shall truly make you know the state of all my businese : and for all thos infinit favors which every [h]our your love gives mee the best satisfacttion must be my affecttion with infinit wishes for your hapines which I can never exepres by my hand or any other way: excepte your faithe wear as your most affectionat sister sends them

E. GRAYE.

I send my most deerst love to my sweete goddaughter with many good wishes for her happie fortune and the like to the rest of your sweette childrin.

Lady Grey's affection for her friend prompted her to write warmly in favour of an aspirer to Anne's hand about this same date. No names are mentioned, but it seems likely that the trusted "berer" in the last letter is the "worthy frind" for whom she pleads :

My deerst sister If I had thought your lines wolde have brought mee this hoples newes of my worthy frinds affecttion I wolde have leffte to have chalinged you

you for the necklect and have desired your lines of another subiett, for I must confes you have handled this so exslently as I knowe not howe to frame any answer to chalinge anythinge you say, for I am in that state you are in but much more unfortunat and I coulde infinitly comend your resolution yf it were any other that offered affecttion : but when I remember whom it is and whatt happines his worthynes promisis I must needs tell you that your to infinit care may take away that happines which myght give much content both to you and yours. God knows you are most deere to mee and so are your sweete childrin in my best wishes and yf any thought did tell my hart this match shoulde be the lest [w]ronge to you or yours, yf it weare for my brother, my hand shoulde never be so false to my hart as to solisit you by my lines to tye you to the lest discontent : but it is needles for mee to plede for him that can with the life of true affection plede for him selfe and to him I leve it with my deerst wishes all may be as happie to you as to my live which is devoted to be everlastingly

       Your affectionat sister
        E. GRAYE.

In spite of so many advocates for a second marriage, we are glad to record Anne continued to "live maister of herself," and remained Anne Newdigate to the end.

The Valley of Death

Lady Grey married again in 1614. Her second husband was a Mr. Bingley, afterwards Sir John Bingley. Her eldest son by Sir John Grey was created Earl of Stamford in 1628.

In this year, 1614, Anne's old friend Sir William Knollys, now Lord Knollys, was appointed Master of the Wards, and she had occasion to appeal to his jurisdiction in regard to pending suits concerning her son's property. Doubtless Anne thought (and rightly as it turned out) that in memory of past times the new Master of the Wards would give every attention to petitions emanating from his former " Gossepp."

Anne's copies of her petitions still exist in two well-thumbed papers in her own handwriting. They are quaintly worded, and are evidently her own composition :

> Right hon^{ble} [she writes] haveing ever bin most bound to yor Los^p though never meriting anythinge, doe presume of the continueance of yor Losp : favoure to me & my Sonne being the Kinge's Ward, now under y^r honores jurisdiction, knowinge yor noble disposition to all & my selfe heretofore liberally tasting thereof, am thereby encouraged in this bold manner to be my Sonn's solicitore to yor Losp : himself being young, not able to be his own intercessor, Thoughe I hope & shalt thinke myself most happie if in time he may attaine to that perfection to be held worthy

The Valley of Death

> worthy to do yor Losp: any service. It hath pleased God since Mr Newd: death (al noble Lord) that sundry sutes & trobles have befallen me in respects of my Sonns estate heare; being amongst a people of strange dispositions, wch I thanke God by this gentleman Mr Chamb: [Chamberlyn*] meanes have well over passed, whoe is my near Neighboure and most willing to Do me al freindly offices in my rightful causes. . . . .

She then enters into particulars of her special grievances, complaining

> that it hath enforced me to call them in to the Court of Wards and to have sutes (being a Woeman and unfitt for these affaires) uppon process sent out of the Court of Wards. 3 Tearmes since [they] have not apeared all to procure mee more troble & charge wch is ever incident to pore unfortunate Woemen in my case. . . . . But since it hath pleased God to place yor Losp: to be my Sonns judge I must confess I shall wth much better comfort seek to defend his right, although it hath ever bin my resolution since it pleased God of his great mercy to bestowe the wardship of my Child uppon me, what in the power of

---

* Probably the owner of Astley Castle of that name, and consequently a near neighbour, Astley Castle being only a mile and a half from Arbury.

The Valley of Death

of my pore endeavoures lieth whereby to settle his estate quietly or keepe it as I found it that I may be blameles shall not be neglected, etc. etc.

This petition evidently met with a favourable response from Lord Knollys. A year later she frames another letter begging him to enforce the payment of the costs he had decreed should be paid her in this suit, which we hope was also successful.

Anne had other cares for her children at this time. She had not overlooked their future marriages, even when they were still in childhood. On more than one occasion she had some correspondence with friends as to an advantageous alliance for her boy. When he was only fourteen years old, she induced a friend, one Robert Phillips, to take a journey into Lincolnshire to make inquiries about a damsel but eleven years of age. Her name is not mentioned, but from the care with which she seems to have been guarded from the eyes of strangers, she must have been of special value as a matrimonial prize. " Pore Robin," as Mr. Phillips calls himself, seems to have fared somewhat badly on this quest:

Good Maddam [he writes] my long and unmannerly staye in yor Ladishippe's house at my last beinge heare is the cause that pen and paper now present the tenour of my embassage in to Lyncollenshyre rather then my person. I have effected what you required, founde the gentell woman to be eleaven yeares old and

The Valley of Death

and no more, neither yet fullye that—no speache of mariadge ether to your nevew or annye other in these partes. She is brought up in her father's house and a pretty gentlewoman as report goes. I sawe her not, but of this I am assured, I might with much more ease have seen all the monuments at Westminster, the lyons in the tower, jack napes and all the beares in parishe garden. Pore Robin was plundged in a cadge so deep that he had rather dive into fower and twenty suche cadges as once he was in then run into it agayne. And yet thanke God I am here; but whilest I live I'll never run more there. God bless me from suche holes. I have a great busines for Thomas Beaumond w[ch] I must needes effecte before I can see Arbery. I laye at his father in lawes at Lyncollen from the 10th daye till Shrove tuesday, and from that tyme at Coleorton till the mundaye after pallme sondaye, and God willinge, I will be with him agayne on wensdaye at nyghte, and there will lye the most parte of this somer and so soone (as possibly I can) I will attend your ladishippe's service (till when) I am ever comendynge yo[r] ladyshippe and al yo[r] prittye checkynges to heaven's protection; not omitting my pritty megge wth her two sharpe teethe and all the rest in generall : Sente from Aldridge this present S[t] George his daye, and remayne your Ladishippe's ever whilest he is his owne to comande

ROBERT PHILLIPS.

The Valley of Death

When I am married forsoothe, then I am at my wyffe's comandes.

But Anne was not destined to live to see her beloved Jack prosperously married, nor even to be released from her anxious wardship.

In the autumn of 1617 she writes to her faithful steward, William Henshawe, who was doing business for her in London, addressing the letter as follows:

> To my good servant Mr Willi: Henshawe at the Signe of the Crowne neare St Martins Gate give these.
> Good Willi:
> Mr Holbitche can not pass without two or three words, he can tell you of our health, al well I thank God but my legg. I pray for yor busines and sone returne. If Mr Thomson be at Whitehall goe see him & Mr Leuston from me wth thanks for al curtesies. I pray you enquire what becomes of Ned Lume my old servant, for I fear Jo: will not be suffycient for the place. At my cousin George Crookes you may heare of him, for he serves my Cousin Boostred's eldest brother. Mr Holbitch is in great hast, you may imagine so by my scribbling. Wth al our remembrances to your good selfe do leave you to God being ever
>
> Your old M^{ris} assured
> A. NEWDIGATE.
>
> Arbery, Oct. 27, 1617.

A month

The Valley of Death

A month later she writes again :

Good Willi:
You have spent a great time in Atendance & never the better, only I can not but beleive there sloweness shewes the poreness of their title. I desire peace if it may be, & so I pray you tell Mr Reede, & commend my love to him & Mr Verney; but if it can not be to Jacke, it shall not be to me.

I was so ill uppon thursday that I could not write to you & am not much better at this time, my legg much trobleing me, althoughe little paine. It is to no purposs to troble Mr Mathias about it, Unless he sawe the manner of it, for I dare applye nothinge unless I had his presence. Mr Mountfort is very carefull, butt knowes nott what to make of it. God's holy wil be done. . . .

Excuse me to al my freinds that at this time I write not to, for I can ill endure to sitt long. Also my eyes are not well able to endure to write. . . .

Am now offerred a match for one of my Daughters, one Mr Kireton. I bade yor uncle write to you to enquire of Mr Willi: Wright, but Jacke must leade the way. I sent you a note of spice & other thinges. I feare yor purse will scarce hold out. If not, I must supply it; but I thinke new fruits will not come in till very neare Christmas, & I neede not any thinge that I have sent for, but a little before the time. I thinke

The Valley of Death

thinke Bousworth the carrier of Nuneaton goeth one jorney more before Christmas. You may enquire of him being now in London, he carryes for three farthinges the pound wch is cheaper then any other.

I pray you gett raphe Hayward to buy for me tow such lanthornes as he bought for me to stick on a wall. Comend me to yor sister & tell hir that the lace I gave hir for Jackes ruffe was butt 15 yeards; if it be not enoughe as I thinke it is not, lett me knowe what wanteth, & I will send it, for there was 3 yeards left behinde.

She then sends excuses to various friends for not answering their letters:

It is my unaptness that hinders. I hope you wil not be long from home, God send us a comfortable meeteing, al my deare children are well I humbly thanke God & comend their loves to you. . . . I pray you comend me to M^{ris} Gresley & thanke her for hir care; intreate that hir Lady may not knowe of the safphir by any meanes, I would have just such A one as that was hir Lady gave me or else none: I will cease yor troble and my owne & leave you to God's blessed keepeing being ever

Yo^r M^{ris} & freind ever assured
A. NEWDIGATE.

I have writt to Sr Franc. Englefield to enquire out a match

match for Jack; put him in minde thereof & entreate my servante Bossone to do as much.

Excuse me to my cosin Ned Fitton. I was about to write to him & Mr Chamb: came & stayed as long as he could see. By my cousin Boustreds horses uppon thursday I wil write if please God. If you can learne the time of any of my friends purposs of being here before you come, I pray you send wordte.

My clock I feare is quite spoiled; it gett 2 howers in 12, & will strike but one in every hower.

There is one more letter written to W. Henshawe four days later, in which she takes advantage of "my cousin Boustred's horses goeing" to send the answers to those "good friends" to whom she could not write before.

The tearme's end [she writes] I hope will send you to us; but if we agree not of peace I pray you knowe of my Cosin Croke, whether in the vacation they can not put A trick uppon us, in respect it is under A colloure for the kinge. Dale gives great words; so doth Anthony Robinson, but I respect them as I do the speakers. We are all well I humbly thanke God. Only my selfe, & that the least matter; my legg I knowe not what to saye of it or do to it but God's blessed wilbe done. I pray you lett Mr Mathias knowe that I have drunke seurby grass this 6 weekes both morninge & after noone & purposs so to do still.

still. I have noe more to troble you with al but to deliver the lace & rebine to yor sister. Jack comends him unto you & bids you tell Willi: Butterton that the lampe had 3 holes in it. A tinker was faine to mend it ; he must furnishe him wth some oile for it. We had from Coventrie & it is so vile that it smells al the house over. Farewell good Willi : comend my love to al my good friends wisheing you A happie jorney & good returne do comite you to God remaineing ever

     Yo^r M^{ris} & assured
Nov^b the 26 friend
  1617   A. NEWDIGATE.

Comend me to Sr Walter Leueson & tell him I hope he will see Arbery in his returne. I heare Sr George Curson went to London this weeke ; if he did I pray you tell him that I take it very unkindly that he would not see me ; I hope he beleives that I would have bin most glad to have sene him at Arbery if he do not he doth me the more wrong tell his La: Daughter so.

These three letters must have been preserved as amongst the last Anne wrote, for early in the following summer (to use her own words) God called her. In the prime of life, being only forty-three years of age, she was taken away, leaving five children to lament the loss of a mother at a critical period of their young lives, the eldest

The Valley of Death

eldest being just twenty and the youngest only eleven years old. Thus she never lived to see her anxious wardship brought to an end; the active brain ceased to work and the loving heart to beat on behalf of the children for whom alone she seemed to live.

In accordance with the directions in her will, she was taken to Harefield to be buried. If she had died at Gawsworth, her desire was to have been laid at rest in the home of her youth. But as she passed away at Arbury her remains now lie beside her husband in the old family burial-place of Harefield. There they rest within the walls of that quaint and picturesque old church, which stands in solitary beauty in an oasis of green meadow land, whilst behind it rises a noble background of fine old trees.

Anne's effigy on the sculptured monument to her husband's memory erected in her lifetime is not a flattering representation of her, and bears little resemblance to her portraits at Arbury, of which there are four.

The latest of these must have been executed about four years before her death. It is a full-length portrait, where she is depicted standing by a table with a fan in her hand. In spite of her large hoop she looks slight in figure, and her countenance is pale and wan. Her gown is of black velvet with a ruff closed at the throat, and the red embroidery of her high-heeled shoes gives the only touch of colour to her dress.

The Valley of Death

Her will, a copy of which, entirely in her own handwriting, is at Arbury, is dated in 1610, the year of her widowhood. Much of the first part is copied from her husband's will, to which she was left sole executrix.
She begins, as was customary at that time, with a profession of her faith :

> In the name of the father and of the sonne and of the holye ghost Amen.
> I dame Anne Newdigate, late wife of Sr John Newdigate Knighte, beinge in health of bodye and in perfect and good memorye thanks be to my mercifull God for the same, at the makinge of this my last Will and Testament wch I ordaine etc. etc.
> First I bequeath my soule into the hand of God my maker & creator and to Jesus Christ my blessed Savio^r and Redimer, and to the Holye Ghoste my blessed sanctifier. . .
> And I bequeath my bodie to the earth from whence it came, desiringe either to bee buried in Herfield churche by my husband, Sr John Newdigate or in Gawesworth Churche by my deare ffather Sr Edward ffitton wthout anie extraordinarye cost, but in a comelie manner, as is fitt, wth some small memorie of mee, as my name, and my husband and ffather's Armes together in some windowe sett. I desire to be buried at Herfield unlesse it shoulde please God I shall dye at Gawesworth since it is God's will that I should outlive

outlive my husbande S^r Jo. Newdigate, and he makinge mee his executrixe, leavinge mee in trust wth his Children, and all that ever he had in the worlde, I hereby charge my Executo^{rs}, as they answere before God at the generall daie of Judgement, that whatsoever shalbe lefte unpformed of his my husband's Will at my death, that it be truelie and faythfullie performed. Item I give to my sonne Jo. Newdigate all chattells, goods, plate, househould stuffe, stocks of cattell quicke or deade that I shall have at the time of my death remayning unbequeathed, my Will being first performed, the remainder to my sonne Jo :

Lady Newdigate then wills certain portions to her daughters and to her second son, who inherits some land as well, and continues :

And whereas out of my deare love to my eldest sonne and for the better upbuilding of his house, I have hereby wholly given and disposed the profitt of his wardshippe and marriage to those uses the sooner to free his landes in Middlesex etc. . . . yet he shall pay each of his sisters Thirtye pounds apeece yearly until they are married or their portions are paid to them . . . . And I earnestlye desire and charge William Whitall as he was left in trust by his M^r my husband S^r Jo : Newdigate and nowe by mee that my boyes may be brought uppe in good learninge and both they and my daughters to be

The Valley of Death

be bred uppe in virteous and godlie lyffe in our Catholick and Protestant Religion to the understandinge of God's holie Will and wayes revealed in his greate compassion and mercie unto us by his divine Gospell and in the true faith of Jesus Christ our onelie Savio^r Redeemer and Mediator, whome I beseache in his abundant mercie make them all five of his chosen elect. And when my boyes are of fittynge learninge and yeares that they maye goe to the Universities and Innes of Courte. And I charge William Withall that my eldest sonne be not married before hee be Sixteene yeares oulde at the least, and not then nor ever against his owne Will and good likinge by anie interest challenged over him by my righte. . . .

She then divides her "gownes, petticoats, jewells" and other valuables amongst her five children. She bequeaths to Richard the bedstead with the yellow velvett canopy and taffata quilt "wch my uncle Francis Fytton gave me." To her mother, who survived her, she left a ring which her father had given her:

Item my Will and desire is to have a fewe playne gould Rings made of tenne or twelve shillinges price wth a pansie being my ffather's Crest, engraven on the outside and two letters for my name enamelled wth blacke on either side the pansie and an inscription wthin to be in lattyn, these wordes followinge: *Death is the begiñinge of life;* and to be delivered unto

The Valley of Death

unto soe manie of my friends as a memorie of my love as I heare nominate :

Amongst those she here mentions is her sister, Mary Polwhele, the date of this portion of her will being shortly after William Polwhele's death and before the Lougher marriage.
The last part was added in 1615, when she goes on :

I nowe make and ordaine my ho^{ble} kinsman Sr Francis Englefield Knighte Baronett, William Whitall and William Henshawe my two servants, my three Executo^{rs}. I did [not] nominate S^r ffrancis till I had spoken wth him who hath promised me to take care of my Children. . . .
In witnesse that this is my Will and Deede I sette my hande the ffower and twentieth of October in the yeare of O^r Lorde 1615.
ANNE NEWDIGATE.

We know no more of the last days of Anne, Lady Newdigate. Her mother and her sister may have been with her at the end, for they both survived her by many years.
On one side of the elaborate monument erected to her father, Sir Edward Fytton, in Gawsworth Church, is the seated figure of his widow, Lady Fytton, her head resting on her hand. Behind her appear her two daughters, Anne and Mary, kneeling, whilst her two sons are in a like attitude in front.

The Valley of Death

Of Mary Lougher we can ascertain only that she was again left a widow in 1636, when she took out letters of administration to her second husband's estate. We are indebted to Mr. Bridgeman for this information and also for the discovery of her will. Had it not been for his unwearied and persistent efforts, we should be without the glimmer of light afforded us by these wills of Polwhele and Mary, and the administration to Lougher. We desire again to record our gratitude to him for the time and pains he has expended in procuring valuable information, and also for his useful criticism of the manuscript of this work.

Mary Lougher's will is dated December 19, 1640, and was proved in the Prerogative Court of the Archbishop of Canterbury on July 5, 1647 : it was proved a second time, before the Probate Court established by Cromwell, on September 22, 1653. The executors appointed by the will were her son, William Polwhele, and her daughter, Elizabeth Lougher, but probate was granted to William Polwhele alone, as "surviving executor."

She bequeaths the lease of Perton to her son, William Polwhele ; the lease of Rinkeston or Rinteston and Killkelly in Pembrokeshire to her daughter, Elizabeth Lougher. She makes bequests to her "little grandchild Ann Gattachree," to her son-in-law, John Gattachree, his wife and three children. She mentions her son-in-law, son-in-law, Robert Chernnock, and gives directions for her burial at Goulsworth (Gawsworth), Co. Chester.

Thus she apparently continued to flourish like a green bay-tree until 1647, the date of her death, when she must have been sixty-nine years old.

In bidding farewell to Mary Fytton, with all the difficulties that obscure her career, we cannot but hope and believe that the brilliant maid of honour, frail though she undoubtedly was, had qualities of heart and soul to enable her to benefit by the love and example of her faithful sister. And as Anne was charitable to her failings to the last, so may we also be.

It may be interesting to jot down here as briefly as possible the main facts in the after life of Anne's five children.

Her eldest son, the much-loved Jack, married early Susanna, daughter of Arnold Luls, a Dutch merchant in London. They had one son, who died in infancy, and when about his mother's age John died himself in the year 1642.

The property then passed to his only brother Richard, a lawyer of great ability and independent honesty. He is known to history in Cromwell's time for having refused to condemn the Earls of Bellasis and Dumfries, with Colonel Halsey and other Royalists who were tried before him at the York Assizes for levying war against the Protector. Judge Newdigate observed that "although by 25 Ed. III. it was high treason to levy war

The Valley of Death

war against the king, he knew of no statute to extend this to a Lord Protector." In consequence of this independence of action he was deprived of his place, but later restored to the Bench by the Commonwealth after the Protectorate was abolished. Later on he was made a baronet by Charles II. He married Julian, daughter of Sir Francis Leigh of Newnham Regis, and had a large family, from one of whom the present family are directly descended, although the male line with the baronetcy became extinct at the beginning of the present century.

Of Anne Newdigate's daughters, the eldest, Mary, nicknamed "Waspsnest" by Sir Richard Leveson, married Edmund Bolton of Granborough, Co. Warwick, but none of her descendants survive, the last of them, a daughter Lettice, having died unmarried in 1693-4. Lettice Bolton was buried in Astley Church, where it is recorded on her monument that she "lived very hansomly upon a narrow fortune; her life was without trouble, and her death without pain."

Anne's second daughter, Lettice Newdigate, died unmarried at the age of twenty.

Anne, the youngest, who was only eleven years old at the time of her mother's death, married Sir Richard Skeffington, Kt., second son of Sir William Skeffington, Bart., of Fisherwick, Co. Stafford, and their son, who married the daughter of Sir John Clotworthy, 1st Viscount Massarene, succeeded to that peerage under the

The Valley of Death

the special remainder of the patent on the death of his father-in-law. Lady Skeffington died when only twenty-nine, and an admiring friend (possibly the "Cousin Boustred" of Lady Newdigate's letters) has perpetuated her memory in a monument erected by him in St. Michael's Church, Coventry.
The inscription is as follows:

> An Elegicall epitaph made upon the death of that mirror of women Ann Newdigate, Lady Skeffington, wife of that true moaneing turtle Sir Richard Skeffington, Kt., & consecrated to her eternal memorie by the unfeigned lover of her vertues, Willm. Bulstrode, Knight.

> Vertue humble, beautie chaste, pious wit,
> Husband's honour, women's glorye, sweetlye knit,
> And all comprised fairelye in this one,
> Sad fate hath here enshrined with this stone.
> Vertue triumph, for thou hast woon the prize;
> Beautie teach women to be chast & wise;
> Make her your patterne of a vertuous life
> Who lived & died a faire unspotted wife.
> She was the mirror of her age and dayes
> And now the subject of transcendent prayse.
> O what a harmonye man's life would be,
> Were women all but neare as good as she.

* * * * *

Obiit Maii 21 ætatis suæ, 29 anno Dni 1637.

Our

The Valley of Death

Our self-imposed task is at an end. Farewell Anne, Dame Newdigate, true daughter, sister, wife and mother. We trust we have done you justice. It has not been for lack of love and admiration if we have failed.

For us, living as we do within the same walls where nearly three hundred years ago, Anne lived, loved and died, where her portraits look down upon us from dining-hall and gallery, our chief heroine's personality has a reality and a fascination which we cannot hope to impart to our readers.

We would, however, hope that Anne's true womanly life may still have an influence for good on the posterity she longed to benefit. May we one and all so learn the true lesson of this life's pilgrimage as to be able to echo from our hearts the last message to her friends of the first Lady Newdigate of Arbury :

"Death is the begiñinge of life."

APPENDIX

Extracts from a list of Anne Newdigate's expenses, showing that she was evidently a visitor to Mary Polwhele at Perton in 1607

Item chickens 14.	0	2	4
It : 6 chickens	0	1	2
It : clarett wine	0	2	0
It : a dozen & halfe of pigeons	0	2	3
It : for rosmarye flowers	0	0	4
It : halfe an elle of lace for lettice	0	2	0
It : to Mr Mathyas	0	10	0
It : broumes	0	0	4
It : to goodwife gardener for her halfe yeare's wages ending at 1607 ou^r La : daye	0	15	0
It : 12 ducklings	0	2	6
It : aquavita	0	1	6
It : 5 couple of rabets	0	3	0
It : to Will : Walker the Joyner	0	0	9
It : tow pans more then the ould	0	5	1
It : Wooden ware for the dogs house	0	1	0

Item a pore

Appendix

Item a pore man	0	0	4
It: a girdle for dicke	0	2	6
It: peirceing 50 pearls	0	1	6
It: makeing Malls ringe	0	1	0
It: a paire of shooes for Jacke . . .	0	1	0
virginall wiers	0	0	4
It: a paire of shoes for myself . . .	0	2	6
It: a paire for lettice	0	1	0
It: the shoemaker's man	0	0	4
12 elles of cloeth weaving & tow dossen of napkins	0	1	0
It: nursse on her goeinge	0	10	0
It: 12 yeards of cobbweb lawn	0	8	0
It: 6 threed laceses	0	0	6

At my being at perton

It: the keeper at Brude parke . . .	0	10	0
It: the keeper's men	0	2	0
It: in the house at perton	0	8	0
It: to my sister for silver chamlett . .	1	0	0
It: Docter Cherriboode	2	0	0
It: at Sr Walter Leueson	0	4	6
It: mending the Coatch	0	2	6
It: my sisters nursse	0	2	0
etc. etc.			

www.ingramcontent.com/pod-product-compliance
Lightning Source LLC
Chambersburg PA
CBHW031445160426
43195CB00010BB/858